Praise for *Six Ways to Study the Bible*

"Trent Butler demonstrates that reverence for Scripture need not preclude asking probing questions about the texts' origin, transmission, and meaning. In an engaging style, Butler welcomes readers into deeper dialogue with the Bible, uncovering the mysteries of study Bible notes and commentators' jargon. By preceding the chapter on devotional study, 'the queen of Bible study,' with guides to textual, literary, historical, exegetical, and theological study, Butler shows how all of these enrich the meaning of the text. Students of the Bible who want to go beyond what other people tell them, but don't know how to start, should grab Butler's book and dig in."

Sandra Hack Polaski, author of A Feminist Introduction to Paul

"*Six Ways to Study the Bible* is a comprehensive tool for any student of the Bible. Outlining six approaches for digging deeper into the text, it provides examples of how to do these and includes exercises the reader can use to practice. An excellent list of Bible study resources is also included. Teachers and students of the Bible in the local church will find this a useful addition to their toolbox of biblical study aids."

Karen Tye, author of Basics of Christian Education

"A good resource for highly motivated laypeople, this book takes readers on an in-depth journey through six different ways of reading the Bible. It will repay its readers with helpful suggestions about these different approaches."

David M. Howard, Jr., Bethel Seminary, St. Paul, Minnesota

"Just as a master craftsman is one who is an expert in working with the tools of his craft, so an educated Bible reader is one who is trained in using the tools of biblical study. In *Six Ways to Study the Bible,* Trent Butler introduces readers to six of the most important tools they should have in their tool belts in order to study the Bible effectively. This slim volume, written by a veteran Bible scholar with the heart of a pastor, would make an excellent preparatory text for church Bible study groups and introductory level college classes."

Ralph K. Hawkins, Kentucky Christian University

To Dr. Paul Redditt,
Friend for Life

Six Ways
to Study
the BIBLE

TRENT C. BUTLER

LUCAS
PARK

BOOKS
ST. LOUIS, MISSOURI

ISBN: 978-1-60350-081-4

Published by Lucas Park Books
www.lucasparkbooks.com

Printed in the United States of America

Contents

Acknowledgments vi

Introduction 1

1. Finding the Text: *Textual Study* 5

2. Finding the Bible's Narrative Genius: *Literary Study* 27

3. Finding the Detailed Meaning: *Exegetical Study* 41

4. Finding What Happened: *Historical Study* 51

5. Finding the Bible's Teaching and Meaning: *Theological Study* 85

6. Finding the Personal Meaning of the Text: *Devotional Study* 101

Conclusion 111

Appendix 1: Bible Tools Worksheet 115

Appendix 2: The Nature of the New Testament 120

Appendix 3: A Brief History of English Bible Translations 122

Appendix 4: Critical Analysis of Some Recent Bible Translations 124

Appendix 5: Selection of Translation Problems 131

Appendix 6: Basic Bible Study Resources 142

Appendix 7: Glossary 150

Acknowledgments

This small volume grows out of a lifetime of ministry in the churches of God's people. Any skills I have in Bible study go back to encouragement and direction from Dr. Don Williams at Southern Baptist Theological Seminary and Dr. Leander Keck at Vanderbilt's Graduate School of Religion. Strong encouragement along the way came from numerous people, especially Dr. Page Kelley, Dr. J. D. W. Watts, Dr. Paul Redditt, and Dr. Marvin Tate. Lessons along the road came from students at the International Baptist Theological Seminary in Rüschlikon, Switzerland, and at Southern Baptist Theological Seminary. Opportunities to develop thoughts in this book came under the tutelage of Johnnie Godwin and in the life of Brentwood Baptist Church, Hopewell Baptist Church, Judson Baptist Church, First Baptist Church Gallatin, College Heights Baptist Church, and First Baptist Church of Hendersonville. My gratitude goes to all those people who have nurtured and encouraged my love for Scriptures through the years.

Of course, the greatest sacrifice for the work on this book came from my dear wife, Mary Martin, and Mary Webb who fended for themselves so often while I retreated to the computer. I also wish to thank Russ White, Pablo Jiménez, and the people at Chalice Press for enduring with me while I completed this manuscript. May the input of all these people be proven worthwhile as this volume goes out to the glory of God.

Introduction

The art of Bible study is learning to ask the right question at the right time.

What questions do you ask as you study the Bible?

Do you ask different questions when you are going to teach a lesson, when you are preparing to be part of a Bible study someone else is teaching, and when you are simply having a quiet devotional reading?

How are these Bible study preparations different?

I want to share with you what I think are the basic tools you should have as you study and the basic information you should be able to put your fingers on. Remember, education is not how much you know, but how quickly you can find what you need to know.

This book will introduce you to six different ways to do Bible study in different settings. You can add, subtract, or combine as you desire. Combining all six will bring you to a comprehensive understanding of the history behind the text, the actual text itself, the nature of the text, and the theological and practical meanings of the text. To do so, we will look at four texts from different time periods, in different styles, from different literary genres, and with different theological purposes. Except for the textual section, the texts used are Joshua 2, Psalm 137, Mark 8, and Philippians 2. In each type of study, you will see examples of how to do the type of study and will be given an exercise for doing the study on one of the passages for yourself.

Textual Study

The most difficult phone calls I had while managing the Bible section at Holman Bible Publishers came from people using the *New International Version* and wanting to know why certain verses were not in their Bible, why even the verse numbers were not there. Textual study of the Bible shows you how to answer such questions.

The resources you have for this are in study Bibles. They come in the footnotes and center or side column references of the Bible and show you that many verses have different readings in different Bible manuscripts. Before you can do serious Bible study, you need to be able to interpret these footnotes and understand what they mean. If you really get serious at this study, you will go to a commentary such as the *Word Biblical Commentary,* the *Anchor Bible,* or the *New International Commentary.* Such resources give you a special section on textual notes.

1

Take a quick glance at five passages using the *King James Version,* the *New American Standard Version,* and one modern version such as the *New International Version,* the *Holman Christian Standard,* the *New Revised Standard,* or the *Revised English Bible.* The passages are Joshua 21:35–38; Genesis 4:8; Judges 6:13–14; Mark 16:9; and 1 John 5:8. What differences do you discover in the translations of these verses? Can you explain why the translations differ or perhaps do not even include these verses? Our first chapter will seek to explain these differences and alert you as to how to discover and understand similar differences in other passages.

Literary Study

An author may use different styles of writing for different audiences in ways that distinguish him or her from any other author. Thus vocabulary and letter style separate Paul's letters from the Letter to the Hebrews. Paul's style in Galatians differs from that which he uses in Philippians because he has different purposes and sees the two churches as needing different approaches.

The basic literary forms are prose and poetry. Poetry includes hymnody, victory songs, laments, prophetic sayings, wisdom poems, historical epics, etc. Prose includes historical narrative, short stories, battle reports, letters, apocalypse, boundary lists, architectural descriptions, instructions, laws, genealogies, etc. Thus we must learn how to distinguish one literary type from another and know what to expect from those styles and literary types.

Exegetical Study

The heart of Bible study comes as we turn to a specific passage and study it word by word, verse by verse, chapter by chapter, and book by book. We must find how to segment a passage out so that we are as sure as possible that we are dealing with what the original writer considered a discrete section of writing. We will see how to find the structure of the passage in relationship to what precedes and follows. We will see how to find the way the passage itself is structured, what communication skills the writer utilizes in the passage, and the major point or points the writer seeks to transmit to the audience. This, in turn, will lead us to find the major theological teaching of the passage and the major response the writer wants the audience to make. Mark 8 will be the central focus for this chapter. Why did Jesus have to try twice before healing a blind man?

Historical Studies

Historical studies provoke more controversy than most any other. They have two points of focus: the time of the writer and the time of the events described. Learning of the time of the writer helps us discover the important themes and situations the writer's audience faces and the author addresses. Such information may lead us to understand the nature of the author's writing style. Historical events may be incorporated into writing in many ways: poetry, biography, historical fiction, propaganda, entertaining narrative, royal annals, or interpretative historical narrative. Each of these writing styles or types can incorporate factual historical details. Each can relate these details in ways that support or oppose certain beliefs or programs. Whatever style, the writer incorporating historical detail has a purpose for using the detail other than simply narrating historical events. This chapter will show how to determine the writer's context and purpose and how the writer uses detail. It will also provide charts the reader can keep close at hand to find needed information about Israelite and Near Eastern history.

Theological Study

No one passage provides all the teaching the Bible seeks to impart on any one subject. Indeed, each passage adds its important nuance to the total biblical teaching. The student of the Bible faces the enormous task of finding other passages in the Bible that deal with the same theme, then fitting them together into a coherent whole that lets us see a theological teaching in its complexity rather than in some simplicity we might impose upon it.

Devotional Study

The "queen" of Bible study is devotional reading. This appears to be the simplest and easiest type of Bible study, but it can be the most careless and dangerous. We cannot deny that at times God speaks directly through the Word to particular needs of God's children. But we must not expect this to happen every time we read the Bible, and we must not let this be the only way we read the Bible. The previous five types of study should inform our devotional reading and help us know what kind of message to expect from a particular portion of Scripture. Of all passages, we will look at Psalm 137 with its gruesome images to determine some limits to place *on*, and some expectations to develop *in*, devotional reading.

CHAPTER 1: Textual

Literary

Exegetical

Historical

Theological

Devotional

Finding the Text

Textual Study

Purpose

To learn how to use basic tools, information, and methods that will equip you to study God's Word with a definite purpose in mind so as to lead to the enrichment of your life with God.

Introduction

The art of Bible study is learning to ask the right question at the right time.

Bible study starts with the text, of course, but which text? Scattered through most of your Bible editions, particularly study Bibles, you find mysterious footnotes that give you important information when you learn how to decipher them. They will show you how different manuscripts (abbreviated "mss") and different early translations of the Bible differ from one another. You need to know enough about these to understand what was happening as the early scribes copied and transmitted the text of the Bible. You also need to be able to come to some reasonable decision as to which text best approximates the earliest text of Scripture. Look at the evidence that follows so you can start to see what we mean when we ask you to "find the text." As we introduce the text, we will also introduce you to some English translations that you may never have used before. You will want to keep a notebook handy as you go through this book, and whenever you study the Bible. Note the following abbreviations:

MT=the *Masoretic Text,* or earliest Hebrew texts we have, coming from Massoretes, or early Jewish scholars, who copied and transmitted the Bible text

LXX=the earliest Greek translation of the Hebrew Bible, done around 250 B.C.E.

TarOnq=*Targum Onqelos*=translation of Hebrew Bible into Aramaic

Vulg=Latin translation by Jerome

SamPent=*Samaritan Pentateuch,* text used by the Samaritan community near Shechem

MSS=manuscripts

The text of the Old Testament is based on two major Hebrew manuscripts from about 1000 C.E.: the Aleppo Manuscript and the Leningrad Manuscript, named for places they have been kept. The Old Testament text is checked for accurate transmission by use of the Septuagint, Dead Sea Scrolls, and other Hebrew manuscripts from after 1000 C.E.; and secondarily by Syriac and Latin Vulgate.

Steps in the Decision

You most likely do not read Greek or Hebrew. To study the Bible with an eye to finding the original text, you must rely on study Bibles and commentaries. But those notes have already confused you. They use too many abbreviations and/or words that do not translate into the way you speak English. So we must expand our vocabulary just a bit to be able to study the evidence. In doing so, we will not try to get technical and exact. We will seek a simple definition that meets your Bible study needs.

Old Testament Manuscripts

Septuagint, abbreviated LXX, and referring to the earliest translation and collection of the Jewish Bible from the Hebrew and Aramaic languages into the Greek language. It contains the Apocrypha, or books about whose authority and inspiration the church has debated for many years (see *Apocrypha* below). The Septuagint quite frequently offers a reading of the Old Testament text that differs significantly from the Hebrew text.

Masoretic Text, abbreviated MT, represents the standard Hebrew text preserved by Hebrew scribes called Massoretes who carefully copied and supplied vowels for a Hebrew text that originally had only consonants.

Leningrad Manuscript B19[A] represents the most complete manuscript of the Hebrew Bible preserved. It dates to 1009 C.E. This text is printed in most modern Hebrew Bibles and is the starting point for textual study.

Vulgate is the standard Latin translation of the Bible and, until Vatican II (1962–65), was the standard Bible read by the Catholic Church. The Vulgate was created because of a lack of uniformity in the earlier Latin translations. In 382 or 383 C.E. Pope Damasus commissioned Jerome to produce a standard Latin translation. At first he translated the Old Testament from the Greek Septuagint. Then about 390 he turned to the Hebrew text and translated it, completing the work—including the apocrypha—about 405. Early in his work, Jerome translated the gospels, but seems not to have finished the New Testament. Through the centuries various groups produced different Latin manuscripts and manuscript traditions. The Council of Trent declared the Latin Bible the official Bible of the Catholic Church. A final text of the Latin Vulgate was produced in 1598. This included much of Jerome's Old Testament work, his gospels, and a sixteenth-century committee's work based on a long history of Latin translations, some older than Jerome and referred to as the Old Latin translation.

The *Bomberg Bible,* named after its publisher, represented the First Rabbinic Bible and was published in Venice in 1516–17.

The *Targums* are the various translations of the Hebrew Bible into Aramaic. These include *Targum Onkelos* of the Pentateuch, which has close ties with the Jewish community in Babylon. It is the most literal of the Targums. It originated in Palestine in the first or early second centuries C.E.

The *Peshitta* or standard *Syriac* translation of the Old Testament first appears in quotations from texts written after 300 C.E. We do not know its origin. The Syriac translation includes several works not included in the Protestant Bible—Wisdom of Solomon, Epistle of Jeremiah, Epistle of Baruch, Baruch, Bel and the Dragon, Susanna, Judith, Ecclesiasticus, 2 *Baruch, 4 Ezra,* 1–4 Maccabees, and Josephus' *Jewish Wars.* Some Psalters contain Psalm 151 (from LXX) and 152–55, now known from the Dead Sea Scrolls.

Dead Sea Scrolls are scrolls of biblical texts and of texts used by the community living in the Jewish community of Qumran. These texts represent the oldest Hebrew texts available to modern scholars. Yet they are very fragmented and contain only a small percentage of the biblical text. See the collection in *The Dead Sea Scrolls Bible* by Abegg, Flint, and Ulrich. In many ways these are the most valuable witnesses to the early Hebrew text.

Samaritan Pentateuch contains the books of Genesis, Exodus, Leviticus, Numbers, and Deuteronomy as preserved by the Samaritan community near Shechem. The date of the community's origin and of its biblical text is a matter of scholarly debate, but it may go back as early as the fall of the Northern Kingdom in 721 B.C.E. However, the oldest copy of their text goes only to about 1200 C.E. The text centers worship life on Shechem rather than Jerusalem or anywhere else.

The New Testament Manuscripts

The New Testament text scholars use is not based on any one manuscript but is a scholarly creation done by examining the almost 5400 different manuscripts of at least part of the Greek New Testament that are available to us. This critical work has to be done because the different manuscripts contain about 300,000 variant readings, most of which can be quickly discarded as normal copying errors. Some of the more important texts include:

Codex Claromontanus from about 350 C.E.—four gospels; ten letters of Paul (probably accidentally omitting Philippians and 1 and 2 Thessalonians); James; 1 and 2 Peter; 1, 2, 3 John; Jude; Barnabas; Revelation; Acts; Shepherd of Hermas; Acts of Paul; and Apocalypse of Peter.

Cheltenham Canon North Africa about 350—four gospels; thirteen letters of Paul; Acts; Revelation; 1,2, 3 John; 1, 2 Peter.

Athanasius, Bishop of Alexandra, 367 C.E.—first to list precisely the twenty-seven books of our New Testament.

Syrian churches had only the **Gospels, Acts, and letters of Paul** until after 400 C.E. Later added **1 Peter, James, 1 John**.

Codex Sinaiticus about 325 had twenty-seven books plus Epistle of Barnabas and Shepherd of Hermas.

Council of Laodicea in 363 C.E. named twenty-six canonical books, omitting Revelation.

Council of Hippo in 393 and Council of Carthage in 397 named twenty-seven books but separated Hebrews from Pauline list.

Note: No ecumenical council of the ancient church ever undertook to define the scope of the canon. Experience of the churches determined the canon. Finally, the church chose those documents considered to be apostolic, catholic (in universal use in the churches), orthodox, and in traditional use.

Footnotes in Your Bible

Once you have learned this information or have it available for quick reference, you are ready to look at the textual footnotes in your Bible.

To do the best textual study you can do, I recommend you should have a copy of the *New King James Bible* (NKJV), the *New English Translation* (NET), and either the *New International Version* (NIV), the *Holman Christian Standard Bible* (HCSB), or the *New Revised Standard Version* (NRSV). If you want to study at an advanced stage, you may want to select a standard commentary that provides textual information. The most complete of these is the *Word Biblical Commentary* series, which supplies so much information you may be overwhelmed. You may want to try volumes from the *New International Commentary on the Old Testament* (NICOT) or the *New International Commentary on the New Testament* (NICNT) or the *New American Commentary* (NAC) or the *Old Testament Library* (OTL) or *New Testament Library* (NTL). The next step forward in textual study would include reference to the *New English Translation of the Septuagint* (NETS).

Before using any of these tools, read the introductory pages in the front to understand the terms being used in the notes, the abbreviations used in the notes, and the types of information available in different types of notes—cross references, textual notes, study notes, charts and graphs, inset notes, etc. Then look to see where the textual notes are situated in the various tools, and find if you have any notes concerning those texts.

Begin the Textual Study

Now you are ready to begin textual study of the text. Follow these steps as you study.

A. English Translation Differences

Look at the translations you are using. Determine what differences appear in the texts. Note these differences in your notebook. Which of these differences appear to reflect simple translation choices rather than textual differences? Write these down in your notebook for further study at a later point.

1. NKJV

2. NET

3. NRSV

4. NIV

5. HCSB

B. Original Language Translation Differences

Look at the notes on the passage in the various tools you are using.

What evidence is available for a different wording in the early translations of the text? Write in your notebook:

1. LXX

2. Vulg

3. Syriac (Peshitta)

4. Targums

C. Making a Decision

1. Do all English translations agree? Note that NKJV is bound by its translation philosophy to maintain textual basis of original King James Version in the New Testament, so its translation may not represent the earliest text, but its extensive footnotes do give us information on which to make decisions.

2. Do the study tools show possible reasons for changes in the text?

   a. Copying error caused by skipping from a word or ending of a word to another word that is the same or has a similar ending.

   b. Copying error caused by copying material twice.

   c. Translation error or change caused by change of culture so that translator did not understand geography or social custom, etc.

   d. Translation change made to avoid "blasphemy" or seeming contradiction in text.

   e. Translation insertion of familiar phrases.

   f. Translation seeking to interpret or clarify the text.

   g. Translation has simplified a difficult text.

   h. Translation has improved literary style or syntax.

   i. One text is more easily derived from the other (when two texts are very similar, but one of them elaborates or expands the information, it is reasonable to see the shorter texts as the source of the longer one).

3. Which reading do you see as preferable or more original?

A look at a couple of examples will illustrate how this type of study works.

Example: Joshua 21:35–38

The Evidence

Jewish Publication Society

Joshua 21:35 Dimnah with its pastures, and Nahalal with its pastures—4 towns.

Joshua 21:36 From the tribe of Gad, Ramoth in Gilead—the city of refuge for manslayers—with its pastures, Mahanaim with its pastures,

Joshua 21:37 Heshbon with its pastures, and Jazer with its pastures—4 towns in all.

Joshua 21:38 All the towns which went by lot to the Merarites, by their clans—the rest of the levitical clans—came to 12 towns.

New King James Version

Joshua 21:35 Dimnah with its common-land, *and* Nahalal with its common-land: four cities;

Joshua 21:36 and from the tribe of Reuben, Bezer with its common-land, Jahaz with its common-land,

Joshua 21:37 Kedemoth with its common-land, and Mephaath with its common-land: four cities;

Joshua 21:38 and from the tribe of Gad, Ramoth in Gilead with its common-land (a city of refuge for the slayer), Mahanaim with its common-land

Holman Christian Standard Bible

Joshua 21:35 Dimnah with its pasturelands, and Nahalal with its pasturelands—four cities.

Joshua 21:36 From the tribe of Reuben, | they gave |: Bezer with its pasturelands, Jahzaha with its pasturelands,

Joshua 21:37 Kedemoth with its pasturelands, and Mephaath with its pasturelands—four cities.

Joshua 21:38 From the tribe of Gad, | they gave |: Ramoth in Gilead, the city of refuge for the one who commits manslaughter, with its pasturelands, Mahanaim with its pasturelands,

The Reasoning

New English Translation Notes

Joshua 21:36–37 are accidentally omitted from a number of significant Hebrew MSS. They are, however, found in some Hebrew MSS, the LXX [Greek translation] and Vulgate [Latin translation].

New King James Version Notes

Following Septuagint and Vulgate (compare 1 Chronicles 6:78–79); Masoretic Text, Bomberg, and Targum omit Joshua 21:36 and 37.

Holman Christian Standard Bible Notes

21:36–37 Some Heb mss omit these vv.

Word Biblical Commentary Text Notes

The major Hebrew tradition does not include vv 36–37, though some later Heb mss do witness them. Such omission, however, makes the arithmetic of v 41 in error. This is probably a case of early haplography [scribal omission of letters or words often caused by skipping from one word to its repetition later in the manuscript]. Reconstruction of the verses is done on the basis of LXX [Greek translation] and 1 Chronicles 6:63–64. The LXX appears to give the earliest reading.

A. English Translation differences:

A first glance shows no significant differences in these texts aside from spellings of geographical names. Yet the notes of the study tools will show us that no one of these translations produces the base Hebrew text represented by the Leningrad manuscript. This reminds us to look for textual notes even where the translations do not reflect differences.

B. Ancient Language Differences (where information is available)

MT—Does not have vv. 36–37

LXX—does have vv. 36–37

Vulg—does have vv. 36–37

Syriac (Peshitta)—Tools used do not mention

Targums—Do not have vv. 36–37.

Bomberg—Does not have vv. 36–37.

C. Making a decision

1. Do all English translations agree? *Yes*

2. Do the study tools show possible reasons for changes in the text?
   a. Copying error caused by skipping from a word or ending of a word to another word that is same or has a similar ending. *Yes—four cities at end of v. 35 to four cities end of v. 37.*
   b. Copying error caused by copying material twice. *No*
   c. Translation error or change caused by change of culture so that translator did not understand geography or social custom, etc. *No*

d. Translation change made to avoid "blasphemy" or seeming contradiction in text. *No*

e. Translation insertion of familiar phrases. *No*

f. Translation seeking to interpret or clarify the text. *No*

g. Translation has simplified a difficult text. *No*

h. Translation has improved literary style or syntax. *No*

i. One text is more easily derived from the other. *Yes—MT derived from LXX in omitting part of LXX rather than LXX adding cities not known in MT.*

3. Which reading do you see as preferable or more original?

Decision: Include vv. 36–37 in the text and explain MT omission as copyist's error moving from one "four cities" to another.

Example: Genesis 4:8

The Evidence

Revised English Bible

Genesis 4:8 Cain said to his brother Abel, 'Let us go out into the country.' Once there, Cain attacked and murdered his brother.

New American Standard, 1995

Genesis 4:8 Cain told Abel his brother. And it came about when they were in the field, that Cain rose up against Abel his brother and killed him.

New International Version

Genesis 4:8 Now Cain said to his brother Abel, "Let's go out to the field." And while they were in the field, Cain attacked his brother Abel and killed him.

God's Word Translation

Genesis 4:8 Cain talked to his brother Abel. Later, when they were in the fields, Cain attacked his brother Abel and killed him.

The Reasoning

Word Biblical Commentary

Sam Pent adds נלכה השדה: "let us go into the field," and this is supported by the ancient versions except TgOnq [Aramaic Targum Onqelos] and S [Syriac], which says "let us go down into the valley." The clause may have been omitted in MT [basic Hebrew text] because of homoioteleuton [scribal error omitting words by skipping from one word to another with a similar ending] with "in the field." The difficulty of MT may have prompted the expansion found in the other texts.

New English Translation Note

The MT has simply "and Cain said to Abel his brother," omitting Cain's words to Abel. It is possible that the elliptical text is original. Perhaps the author uses the technique of aposiopesis, "a sudden silence" to create tension. In the midst of the story the narrator suddenly rushes ahead to what happened in the field. It is more likely that the ancient versions (Samaritan Pentateuch, LXX, Vulgate, and Syriac), which include Cain's words, "Let's go out to the field," preserve the original reading here. After writing אָחִיו *achiyv* "his brother"), a scribe's eye may have jumped to the end of the form בַּשָּׂדֶה (*basadeh*, "to the field") and accidentally omitted the quotation. In older phases of the Hebrew script the sequence יו (*yod-vav*) on אָחִיו is graphically similar to the final ה(*he*) on בַּשָּׂדֶה ("in the field").

Holman Christian Standard Bible Note

Sam, LXX, Syr, Vg; MT omits *Let's go out to the field.*

The Decision

1. Look at the translations you are using. Determine what differences appear in the texts.

   Some translations have Cain's words; others do not.

   Note these differences in your notebook.

   Which of these differences appear to reflect simple translation choices rather than textual differences? *None*

   Check these off in your notebook for further study at a later point.

2. Look at the notes on the passage in the various tools you are using. What evidence is available for a different wording in the early translations of the text? Write in your notebook:

A. English Translation differences:

   NKJV—*No quotation*
   Now Cain talked with Abel his brother; and it came to pass, when they were in the field, that Cain rose up against Abel his brother and killed him.

   NET— *Quotation supplied from LXX;* Use of "attacked" to translate literal "rose up."

Cain said to his brother Abel, "Let's go out to the field." While they were in the field, Cain attacked his brother Abel and killed him.

NRSV— *Quotation supplied from LXX;*
Cain said to his brother Abel, "Let us go out to the field." And when they were in the field, Cain rose up against his brother Abel, and killed him.

NIV— *Quotation supplied from LXX;* Use of "attacked" to translate literal "rose up."
Now Cain said to his brother Abel, "Let's go out to the field." And while they were in the field, Cain attacked his brother Abel and killed him.

HCSB—*Quotation supplied from LXX;* Use of "attacked" to translate literal "rose up."
Cain said to his brother Abel, "Let's go out to the field." And while they were in the field, Cain attacked his brother Abel and killed him.

B. Ancient Language Differences (where information is available)

Samaritan Pentateuch—Has quote

LXX—Has quote

Vulg—Has quote

Syriac (Peshitta)—Has quote

Targum—Has quote

C. Making a decision

1. Do all English translations agree? *No*

2. Do the study tools show possible reasons for changes in the text? *Yes*
   a. Copying error caused by skipping from a word or ending of a word to another word that is the same or has a similar ending.
      Skipped from field of quotation to field in next clause
   b. Copying error caused by copying material twice. *No*
   c. Translation error or change caused by change of culture so that translator did not understand geography or social custom, etc. *No*
   d. Translation change made to avoid "blasphemy" or seeming contradiction in text. *No*

e. Translation insertion of familiar phrases. *No*

f. Translation seeking to interpret or clarify the text.

   Possible; scribal tradition may have seen very early need to supply quotation to make text clear

g. Translation has simplified a difficult text.

   Possible explanation

h. Translation has improved literary style or syntax. *No*

i. One text is more easily derived from the other.

   Either text could be derived from other through addition or through copying error

3. Which reading do you see as preferable or more original?

Decision: Difficult. MT without quote represents more difficult reading, which is often the best reading. MT could be seen as using literary tool to let reader supply quote in moment of silence or may have simply intended to say they were in conversation when the attack occurred. More likely, a simple copyist's error led to omission of quote quite early in text history. Read the quote in the text but with some reservation.

Example: Judges 16:13–14

The Evidence

New International Version

Judges 16:13 Delilah then said to Samson, "Until now, you have been making a fool of me and lying to me. Tell me how you can be tied." He replied, "If you weave the seven braids of my head into the fabric [on the loom] and tighten it with the pin, I'll become as weak as any other man." So while he was sleeping, Delilah took the seven braids of his head, wove them into the fabric

Judges 16:14 and tightened it with the pin. Again she called to him, "Samson, the Philistines are upon you!" He awoke from his sleep and pulled up the pin and the loom, with the fabric.

Jewish Publication Society

Judges 16:13 Then Delilah said to Samson, "You have been deceiving me all along; you have been lying to me! Tell me, how could you be tied up?" He answered her, "If you weave seven locks of my head into the web."

Judges 16:14 And she pinned it with a peg and cried to him, "Samson, the Philistines are upon you!" Awaking from his sleep, he pulled out the peg, the loom, and the web.

New King James Version

Judges 16:13 Delilah said to Samson, "Until now you have mocked me and told me lies. Tell me what you may be bound with." And he said to her, "If you weave the seven locks of my head into the web of the loom"—

Judges 16:14 So she wove *it* tightly with the batten of the loom, and said to him, "The Philistines *are* upon you, Samson!" But he awoke from his sleep, and pulled out the batten and the web from the loom.

Holman Christian Standard Bible

Judges 16:13 Then Delilah said to Samson, "You have mocked me all along and told me lies! Tell me how you can be tied up." He told her, "If you weave the seven braids on my head with the web of a loom—"

Judges 16:14 She fastened the braids with a pin and called to him, "Samson, the Philistines are here!" He awoke from his sleep and pulled out the pin, with the loom and the web.

The Reasoning

New English Translation Note

The MT of vv. 13b–14a reads simply, "He said to her, 'If you weave the seven braids of my head with the web.' And she fastened with the pin and said to him." The additional words in the translation, "and secure it with the pin, I will become weak and be like any other man.' **16:14** So she made him go to sleep, wove the seven braids of his hair into the fabric on the loom," which without doubt represent the original text, are supplied from the ancient Greek version. (In both vv. 13b and 14a the Greek version has "to the wall" after "with the pin," but this is an interpretive addition that reflects a misunderstanding of ancient weaving equipment. The Hebrew textual tradition was accidentally shortened during the copying process.) A scribe's eye jumped from the first instance of "with the web" to the second, causing him to leave out inadvertently the intervening words.

Word Biblical Commentary

Words in brackets reconstructed from the LXX, "if you should knock with a pin (or peg) into the wall, I will be weak as one of the men." OL [Old Latin] reads, "If you take apart the seven locks of my head and you lay the warp of a web and you lay bare my hairs in it as if the web is covered over, I will become weak."

LXX[A] [a Greek manuscript of Judges] reads "and Delilah put him to sleep and began to weave the locks of hair of his head with the extension and nailed the pen into the wall." The reference to nailing into the wall seems to be a Gk. interpretation from normal usage of the Gk. verbs. These clauses are apparently missing from the MT through homoioteleuton [skipping to similar ending]. LXX[B] [a second Greek manuscript] reads v 14a as "and in his sleeping Delilah took the seven chains of his head and wove in the warp and fastened the pin into the wall." OL translates, "And Delilah made him sleep and she took apart the seven hairs of his head with fear, and she went out in the length of the room, and she fixed it in pins and she said to him, 'Foreigners are upon you, Samson.' And he rose up from his sleep, and he plucked out the pins with the loom and the 'division' [of his hair?] and his strength was not known."

New International Version Note

"'If you weave the seven braids of my head into the fabric on the loom and tighten it with the pin, I'll become as weak as any other man.' So while he was sleeping, Delilah took the seven braids of his head, wove them into the fabric and"—Some Septuagint manuscripts; Hebrew *"I can if you weave the seven braids of my head into the fabric on the loom."* So she…

Decision

Here the reader is invited to go through the steps and make the decision.

A. English Translation differences:

     NKJV

     NET

     NRSV

     NIV

     HCSB

B. Ancient Language Differences (where information is available)

     LXX

     Vulg

Syriac (Peshitta)

Targums

C. Making a decision

1. Do all English translations agree? Note that NKJV is bound by its translation philosophy to maintain textual basis of original *King James Version* in the New Testament, so its translation may not represent the earliest text, but its extensive footnotes give us information on which to make decisions.

2. Do the study tools show possible reasons for changes in the text?

   a. Copying error caused by skipping from a word or ending of a word to another word that is the same or has a similar ending.

   b. Copying error caused by copying material twice.

   c. Translation error or change caused by change of culture so that translator did not understand geography or social custom, etc.

   d. Translation change made to avoid "blasphemy" or seeming contradiction in text.

   e. Translation insertion of familiar phrases.

   f. Translation seeking to interpret or clarify the text.

   g. Translation has simplified a difficult text.

   h. Translation has improved literary style or syntax.

   i. One text is more easily derived from the other.

3. Which reading do you see as preferable or more original?

Example: Mark 16:8

The Evidence

See text with brackets, parentheses, and/or footnotes in your translations.

The Reasoning

New English Translation

The gospel of Mark ends at this point [v. 8] in some witnesses, including two of the most respected [Greek] MSS. The following shorter ending is found in some MSS: "They reported briefly to those around Peter all that they had been commanded. After these things Jesus himself sent out through them, from the east to the west, the holy and imperishable preaching of eternal salvation. Amen." This shorter ending is usually included with the longer ending [at least one witness], however, ends at this point. Most MSS include the longer ending (vv. 9–20) immediately after v. 8 [but MSS evidence also shows a different shorter ending between vv. 14 and 15]. Jerome and Eusebius knew of almost no Greek MSS that had this ending. Several MSS have marginal comments noting that earlier Greek MSS lacked the verses, while others mark the text with asterisks or obeli (symbols that scribes used to indicate that the portion of text being copied was spurious). Internal evidence strongly suggests the secondary nature of both the short and the long endings. Their vocabulary and style are decidedly non-Markan. All of this evidence strongly suggests that as time went on scribes added the longer ending, either for the richness of its material or because of the abruptness of the ending at v. 8. (Indeed, the strange variety of dissimilar endings attests to the probability that early copyists had a copy of Mark that ended at v. 8, and they filled out the text with what seemed to be an appropriate conclusion. All of the witnesses for alternative endings to vv. 9–20 thus indirectly confirm the Gospel as ending at v. 8.) Because of such problems regarding the authenticity of these alternative endings, 16:8 is usually regarded as the last verse of the gospel of Mark. There are three possible explanations for Mark ending at 16:8: (1) The author intentionally ended the Gospel here in an open-ended fashion; (2) the Gospel was never finished; or (3) the last leaf of the ms was lost prior to copying. The first explanation is the most likely due to several factors, including (a) the probability that the Gospel was originally written on a scroll rather than a codex (only on a codex would the last leaf get lost prior to copying); (b) the unlikelihood of the ms not being completed; and (c) the literary power of ending the Gospel so abruptly that the readers are now drawn into the story itself. E. Best aptly states, "It is in keeping with other parts of his Gospel that Mark should not give an explicit account of a conclusion where this is already well known to his readers" (*Mark*, 73). The readers must now ask themselves, "What will I do with Jesus? If I do not accept him in his suffering, I will not see him in his glory."

Double brackets have been placed around this passage to indicate that most likely it was not part of the original text of the gospel of Mark. In spite of this, the passage has an important role in the history of the transmission of the text, so it has been included in the translation.

Word Biblical Commentary

Although scholars are almost evenly divided over the question of whether v 8 was the original conclusion of the gospel of Mark, almost all regard both the so-called Long Ending (i.e., vv 9–20) and the Short Ending as textually spurious. Most think the longer passage is a late secondary conflation of traditions found in Matthew, Luke, John, and Acts, enriched with a few legendary details… [I]t is much more probable that the ending is not original, even if it does preserve some details that may have been part of the original ending.

Parts of Mark's long ending appear to be based on various elements found in the other Gospels and Acts. Some of the most obvious elements are as follows:

v. 11: Lack of belief (cf. Luke 24:11)

v. 12: Two on the road (cf. Luke 24:13–35)

v. 14: Reproach for unbelief (cf. John 20:19, 26)

v. 15: Great Commission (cf. Matthew 28:19)

v. 16: Salvation/Judgment (cf. John 3:18, 36)

v. 17: Speaking in tongues (cf. Acts 2:4; 10:46)

v. 18: Serpents and poison (cf. Acts 28:3–5)

v. 18: Laying hands on the sick (cf. Acts 9:17; 28:8)

v. 19: Ascension (cf. Luke 24:51; Acts 1:2, 9)

v. 20: General summary of Acts

The material appears to be abbreviated and/or summarized from these sources.

New King James Version Notes

Verses 9–20 are bracketed in NU-Text as not original. They are lacking in Codex Sinaiticus and Codex Vaticanus, although nearly all other manuscripts of Mark contain them.

The Decision

Scholarship is virtually unanimous in seeing 16:9–20 as a later addition to the text by scribes who were not satisfied with the ending at verse 8. Textual evidence highly favors verse 8 as the original ending unless early manuscripts lost that ending. If that is the case, then we do not have the original ending of Mark but still have a sufficient word to show us the power of the resurrection of Jesus.

Example: 1 John 5:8

The Evidence

New King James Version

1 John 5:7 For there are three that bear witness in heaven: the Father, the Word, and the Holy Spirit; and these three are one.
1 John 5:8 And there are three that bear witness on earth: the Spirit, the water, and the blood; and these three agree as one.

New English Translation (NET)

1 John 5:7 For there are three that testify,
1 John 5:8 the Spirit and the water and the blood, and these three are in agreement.

New American Standard Bible 1995

1 John 5:7 For there are three that testify:
1 John 5:8 the Spirit and the water and the blood; and the three are in agreement.

Revised English Bible

1 John 5:7 [-8] In fact there are three witnesses, the Spirit, the water, and the blood, and these three are in agreement.

The Reasoning

New King James Version Notes

NU-Text and M-Text omit the words from *in heaven* (1 John 5:7) through *on earth* (verse 8). Only four or five very late manuscripts contain these words in Greek.

New American Standard Notes

"the Spirit and the…"—A few late mss add…*in heaven, the Father, the Word, and the Holy Spirit, and these three are one. And there are three that testify on earth, the Spirit*

Word Biblical Commentary

Between vv 7 and 8, after, "those bearing witness"), six Gr MSS introduce a gloss which the AV [Authorized version=King James] translates as, "in heaven, the Father, the Word, and the Holy Ghost: and these three are one. (8) And there are three that bear witness in earth."

The earliest of these Gr witnesses, all of which depend on an earlier Latin tradition, can be dated to the twelfth century. The OL is the only ancient version to include the words, and then with variations between the MSS; but, although the evidence is not entirely clear, the passage seems to be unknown in these texts before the eighth century. It does not appear in Jerome's definitive edition of the Vg [Vulgate] (*circa* AD 404), even if some other MSS of the Vg contain the addition. The earliest extrabiblical writer to show knowledge of the section is the Spanish heretic Priscillian (who died *circa* AD 385), when quoting from this part of John in his Latin "Book of Apology" (*Liber Apologeticus*). None of the Greek Fathers quotes the words. Despite this slight MSS attestation the inclusion remained in the Vg and also survived in the AV. In most modern translations the words have disappeared from the text altogether.

The section, which in any case interrupts the thought of the passage, is clearly an interpolation. Presumably it represents an attempt on the part of those who, in the third and fourth centuries, were preoccupied with understanding the doctrine of the Trinity, to explain this text in a trinitarian manner. What may have begun life as a marginal gloss in a Latin MSS then became incorporated in the text, and was eventually translated back into Gr in some Gr MSS. For similar additions to the Latin text of 1 John see 2:17 and 5:20.

The Decision

1. Look at the translations you are using. Determine what differences appear in the texts. Note these differences in your notebook.

NKJV has a second part to v. 7 and a first part to v. 8 that do not appear in other translations.

Which of these differences appear to reflect simple translation choices rather than textual differences? *None*

2. Look at the notes on the verse in the various tools you are using. What evidence is available for a different wording in the early translations of the text. Write in your notebook:

7b and 8a appear only in late Latin and Greek mms; NKJV translation philosophy forces choice to use the late texts

A. English Translation differences:

NKJV—*Adds 7b and 8a*

NET—*Does not have 7b and 8a*

NRSV—*Does not have 7b and 8a*

NIV—*Does not have 7b and 8a*

HCSB—*Does not have 7b and 8a*

B. Ancient Language Differences (where information is available)

Earliest texts do not have these verses

C. Making a decision

1. Do all English translations agree?

No, because NKJV is bound by its translation philosophy to use text of original KJV so its translation may not represent the earliest text, but its footnotes show that only a few mss have the reading they follow.

2. Do the study tools show possible reasons for changes in the text?

   a. Copying error caused by skipping from a word or ending of a word to another word that is the same or has a similar ending. *No*

   b. Copying error caused by copying material twice. *No*

   c. Translation error or change caused by change of culture so that translator did not understand geography or social custom, etc. *No*

   d. Translation change made to avoid "blasphemy" or seeming contradiction in text. *No*

   e. Translation insertion of familiar phrases. *Yes*

   f. Translation seeking to interpret or clarify the text.
       Yes by inserting doctrine of Trinity into text

   g. Translation has simplified a difficult text. *No*

   h. Translation has improved literary style or syntax. *No*

   i. One text is more easily derived from the other.

7b and 8a reflect theological interpretation in light of Trinitarian debate in early church and have been awkwardly added to Greek text

3. Which reading do you see as preferable or more original?

Addition in NKJV has very little textual support and is obviously later theological addition

Decision: Read text without 7b and 8a.

Next Steps

Now you have watched someone else work to determine the text to interpret, so it is your time to try. Work on the texts above and make sure you agree with the answers given. If not, why not? If you want to take this a step further, compare 2 Kings 20 and Isaiah 38 or work through 1 Samuel 11:6–10 or John 7:53 to 8:11 or Matthew 6:13.

As you study these critical textual matters, remember the amazing reality of the preservation of these ancient texts through time, the hard work copyists did to keep the texts alive for generation after generation, and the amazing agreement of most textual witnesses to the greater part of the biblical text. Textual study is necessary for any kind of true depth Bible study, but such textual study should drive you to greater appreciation for the text we have, not to any type of doubt or fear concerning the authority of the text for your life under God.

Reflection Arising from Textual Study

Textual study is more than a detective opportunity to find answers to textual questions. Textual study calls on you for theological reflection as to what you have learned about the nature of holy Scripture by employing the method of study. Write answers to the following questions in your notebook.

1. How do you explain how textual differences arose? How do you explain how so much of the text does not come under question?

2. How do you incorporate the textual evidence you have studied into a personal understanding of the authority and inspiration of the Bible as God's Word?

3. What conclusions do you draw from the fact that God trusted human scribes to copy and preserve the Holy Scriptures?

As you study the Bible, you will want to use various translations. The descriptions in Appendix 4 should help you see the translation philosophies behind each translation. This will help you choose a translation to use in various situations such as devotional study, introductory reading of the Bible, or serious Bible word study.

Finding the Bible's Narrative Genius

Literary Study

The Bible is a collection of pieces of outstanding world literature. The human authors penned literary pieces that have won the right to be called literary masterpieces in comparison to Homer, Shakespeare, Dante, and all the great literary writers of our world. Such statements do not stand in contrast to divine inspiration. They stand in concert with the church's testimony to God's divine intervention in producing and preserving Scripture. Such inspiration did not produce a mystical book only a few can read. It did not produce a book like the muse's "inspiration" produced Shakespeare's comedies and dramas. Indeed, God-gifted and inspired writers produced pieces of literature that even secular writers proclaim as among the literary giants of world history.

This means the biblical authors used many of the same literary tools that we find in other great literature. To fully understand biblical writings, we must ask the same questions the literary reviewer asks of other great literary works. Among these questions are:

1. How do you tell if a piece of literature in English is poetry or prose? Does identifying a work as poetry make any difference as to how you interpret the writing? How do you recognize Hebrew poetry? What difference does it make in your interpretation if you discover a piece of Hebrew or Greek poetry in the Bible?

2. What are the components of a biblical narrative? How does a biblical writer create a point of tension and then reach resolution in the narrative?

3. What types of literature appear in the Bible? What difference does it make whether you recognize the type of literature or not? Can you miss the major point of a narrative because you do not see that the writer is doing something entirely different from what you expect? When you decide to study an Old Testament prophetic book, what kinds of materials do you expect to find? Do you find these in Jonah? Why not? Is Jonah in some way an ironic parody on prophecy? What are we supposed to learn from a book that shows you how not to be a prophet?

4. How do you determine the starting and ending points of a section of literature? What marks the transition from one section to another? What is the importance of finding these beginning and finishing markers?

5. How do you discover a literary piece's major themes, featured theological issues, basic outline, and key thematic verses?

6. How does a writer's characterization of a person relate to the actual complexity of that person's identity?

Literary study seeks to find an answer to the above questions and many others. A set procedure helps you begin to answer these questions.

1. Choose a passage for study. We will arbitrarily list four passages: Joshua 2; Psalm 137; Mark 8:22–26; Philippians 2.

2. Find the opening structural marker separating the chosen passage from what precedes. Find the closing structural marker separating the passage from what follows.

3. Read as many translations as possible (four or five is good) to detect significant translation differences. Use a concordance to determine as far as possible why the differences exist; use footnotes to see if the translation has followed a different manuscript.

4. Outline the chronological line the passage presents—watch for flashbacks or predictions or other elements out of chronological sequence.

5. Determine the kind of literature you are dealing with—that is, the type or genre of the literary piece: poetry or prose; fiction or nonfiction; letter, list, story, report, speech, historical narrative, etiology, genealogy, etc. (Note glossary at end of the book.)

6. Select the key verse that shows the intent of the passage.

7. Outline the development of the basic theme or issue in the passage—
   in narrative literature, go from the statement of the problem to its
   resolution, if it is resolved here.

Example: Joshua 2

STEP ONE: The Passage

Author's Translation from *Word Biblical Commentary*, vol. 7, 24–25.

1:16 They answered Joshua, "Everything which you have commanded us, we will do; everywhere you send us, we will go. 17 According to all the way in which we have obeyed Moses, so we will obey you. Only let Yahweh your God be with you just as he was with Moses. 18 Every man who rebels against your order and does not obey to the last detail your words, which you command us, shall be put to death. Only may you have conviction and courage."

2:1 Then Joshua, the son of Nun, sent out from Shittim two men for secret spying, saying, "Go, see the land and Jericho." So they went and came to the house of a woman, a prostitute. Her name was Rahab. They bedded down there. 2 It was then reported to the king of Jericho, "Two men have just come here tonight from the Israelites to spy out the land." 3 So the king of Jericho sent to Rahab, "Bring out the men who have come to you, who have come to your house, for they have come to spy out all the land." 4 The woman took the two men and hid them. She said, "Certainly you are right. The men came to me, but I did not know from where they came. 5 When the gate was to close at dark, the men went out. I do not know where the men went. Pursue quickly after them because you can overtake them."

6 Then she brought them up to the roof and concealed them in the flax stalks arranged by her on the roof. 7 Meanwhile, the men pursued after them the way of the Jordan on the crossings, but they had closed the gate just as the pursuers went out after them. 8 They were still not bedded down when she came up to them upon the roof. 9 She said to the men, "I know that Yahweh has given to you all the land and that the dread of you (pl) has fallen on us and that all the inhabitants of the land melt away before all of you, 10 for we have heard that Yahweh dried up the waters of the Reed Sea before you when you came out of Egypt and what you did to the two kings of the Amorites who were beyond the Jordan, to Sihon and to Og whom you (pl) committed to the ban. 11 We heard and our heart melted. Spirit remains in no one because of you (pl), for Yahweh your God it is who is God in heaven above and on the earth below. 12 Now make an oath with me in the name of Yahweh. Since I have treated you (pl) graciously, you (pl), yes you (pl), shall deal

graciously with the house of my father. You (pl) shall give me a true sign. 13 You (pl) shall save alive my father and my mother and my brothers and my sisters and all that belongs to them. You shall deliver our lives from death."

14 The men said to her, "Our lives are in place of yours even to death! If you (pl) do not report this business of ours, then when Yahweh gives us the land, we will treat you with kindness and faithfulness."

15 Then she let them down with rope through the window because her house was in the city wall. Thus she was living in the wall. 16 She said to them, "Go to the mountain lest the pursuers encounter you. Hide yourselves there three days until the pursuers return. Afterwards, you may go your way."

17 The men said to her, "We are exempt from this oath of yours which you have caused us to swear. 18 Right as we are entering the land, this cord of scarlet thread you shall tie in the window from which you let us down. Your father, mother, brothers, and all the house of your father you shall gather to yourself to the house. 19 Everyone who shall go out from the doors of your house to the outside shall have his blood on his own head. We shall be exempt. But everyone who is with you in the house, his blood shall be on our head if a hand should be laid upon him. 20 But if you report this business of ours, then we will be exempt from your oath which you caused us to swear."

21 She said, "According to your words, thus it shall be." Then she sent them away, and they left. And she tied the scarlet cord in the window. 22 So they left and came to the mountain. They remained there three days until the pursuers had returned. The pursuers searched in all the way, but found nothing. 23 The two men returned and came down from the mountain. They passed over and came to Joshua, the son of Nun, and reported to him all their findings. 24 They told Joshua that Yahweh had given into our hand the whole land. "All the inhabitants of the land even melt before us." 3:1 Joshua got up early in the morning. They set out from Shittim and came to the Jordan, he and all the sons of Israel. They spent the night there before they passed over.

STEP TWO: Opening and Closing Markers

The conversation between Joshua and the eastern representatives concludes with a quotation that closes the negotiations: "Only may you have conviction and courage." The next segment opens in 2:1 with a change of location, a new cast of characters, and new instructions from Joshua. In 2:24 the spies report back in a way that completes their mission, though a type of appendix to this story will appear in 6:17–25. The new segment appears in 3:1 with a change of time, a change of characters, and a change of mission. These structural changes determine 2:1–24 as the structural limits of the passage. In this occasion such limits coincide with those of the English chapter markings, but often this is not the case.

STEP THREE: Translation Variances

Verse 1—*New Living Translation* (NLT) does not translate "son of Nun" and translates the Hebrew place name Shittim as Acacia Grove instead of transliterating it. NLT adds "on the other side of the Jordan River" for clarity.

Verse 1—Author's Translation (AT) in *Word Biblical Commentary* includes the Hebrew text emphasis on "woman," often omitted as redundant in English translations, and uses "bedded down" as a more literal and striking translation of the Hebrew.

Verse 1—*New King James Version* (NKJV)—Uses Acacia Grove.

Verse 1—*Holman Christian Standard Bible* (HCSB)—Uses Acacia Grove; translates "woman."

Verse 1—*God's Word* (GW)—Adds "city of" to more clearly identify Jericho as part of the land.

Here the different translation techniques show efforts to clarify and, to an extent, simplify the original text without major translation issues. Using "woman" and "bedded down" helps the reader see the beginning of narrative irony that will follow. The reader can perform this step on each verse.

STEP FOUR: Chronological Movement

Verse 1

Joshua and men at Shittim (Acacia Grove)

Spies bedded down at house of Rahab, the prostitute

Verse 2

Report made to royal palace

Verse 3

Messengers question Rahab

Verses 4–5

Rahab hides spies (apparently out of chronological order since she could not interrupt talk with messengers to run to roof and hide spies)

Interrogation continues between messengers and Rahab with clever prostitute outwitting royal messengers

Messengers leave on wild goose chase

Verse 6

> Rahab hid spies in flax on roof; notice most translations use past perfect tense here (Is this a flashback repeating information from v. 4?)

Verse 7

> Messengers move to Jordan

> Closing of gate (flashback to v. 5)

Verse 8

> Not bedded on the roof (compare v. 1)

Verses 9–13

> Rahab's negotiations with spies

Verse 14

> Spies counter-negotiation with Rahab

Verses 15–16

> Rahab lets spies down a rope out the window and gives instructions to hide three days (compare 1:11; 2:22; 3:2, 5)

Verses 17–20

> Spies set forth conditions for freedom

Verses 21–22

> Rahab agrees to terms and dismisses spies

Verses 23–24

> Spies return and report to Joshua, quoting prostitute

STEP FIVE: Genre or Type of Literature

The piece is prose, not poetry, since it shows no signs of Hebrew poetic parallelism (see discussion of Ps. 137).

The piece is basically a series of short conversations and negotiations. The basic elements include:

1. Selection of spies (1a)

2. Instructions for spies (1b)

3. Mission of spies with irony of beds with prostitute (1c)

4. Narrative tension: royal messengers (1d–3)

5. Narrative resolution: spies hidden, messengers sent away (4–7)

6. Renewed narrative tension (plot complication): prostitute's demands (8–13)

7. Apparent narrative resolution: spies agreement and prostitute's escape plans (14–16)

8. Renewed narrative tension (plot complication): dangling spies amend agreements (17–20)

9. Final resolution: prostitute agrees (21a)

10. Denouement: spies escape, hide, return, and report.

The basic genre or literary type here is that of a simple spy story (compare Numbers 13—14; 21:32–35; Deuteronomy 1:19–46; Joshua 14:7–8; Judges 18) now complicated by the conversations with the prostitute. The simple form would have spies chosen, instructed, sent on mission, gain necessary information, and report back. This would normally serve as the prelude to a battle report as seen in 7:2–3, where the following report registers an Israelite loss, not victory.

STEP SIX: Key Teaching Verse(s)

The key verse of a spy story would normally be the final report with the evidence for thinking one could win the battle and so should enter into battle. Joshua 2 in its expanded battle report style offers several key verse possibilities: 9–11, 14, 19–20, 24. The first set of verses is probably the central statement of the story, but the interesting discovery is that all the possible selections contain the same basic theme: Yahweh has given Israel the land. Israel is ready for battle because Yahweh owns the land and has given it to Israel, as God's children, for an inheritance. They must now obediently take what God has given.

STEP SEVEN: Narrative Theme

The theme begins in verse 1 with mention of land and special reference to Jericho. This is not only the theme of this chapter but one of the major themes of the book as a whole. The theme of land is closely tied to the theme of obedience, placed here without resolution in the theme of insider versus outsider—that is, who may belong to Israel. This may be cast in terms of politics (our side versus the enemies), in terms of nationality (Israelites versus Canaanites), or in terms of profession (accepted professions versus unacceptable ones, such as a prostitute).

The theme is related with great irony: a nation promised the land by God sends out spies to see if they can take it, a prostitute as heroine, royal messengers outsmarted by a prostitute they evidently know well, spies repeatedly bedding down in a house of prostitution, vagabond spies able to outwit king's servants, Israel's confession of faith in the mouth of a prostitute, men negotiating while hanging outside the city wall on a rope, and spies finally able to "outnegotiate" the woman and determine the conditions of her family's freedom.

Here is biblical storytelling at its best. The basic spy form has no real tension, simply repeating the movements and findings of the spies. Here tension and conflict arise as royal messengers become involved, a prostitute mediates, and prostitute and spies exchange freedom plans and oaths of obedience. Along the line of narrative tension arises the line of social, political, and religious tension: Is there room for a pious prostitute in Israel?

Example: Psalm 137

STEP ONE: The Passage

(Tanakh of Jewish Publication Society)

Psalm 136:26 Praise the God of heaven, His steadfast love is eternal.

Psalm 137:1 By the rivers of Babylon, there we sat, sat and wept, as we thought of Zion.

Psalm 137:2 There on the poplars we hung up our lyres,

Psalm 137:3 for our captors asked us there for songs, our tormentors, for amusement, "Sing us one of the songs of Zion."

Psalm 137:4 How can we sing a song of the LORD on alien soil?

Psalm 137:5 If I forget you, O Jerusalem, let my right hand wither;

Psalm 137:6 let my tongue stick to my palate if I cease to think of you, if I do not keep Jerusalem in memory even at my happiest hour.

Psalm 137:7 Remember, O LORD, against the Edomites the day of Jerusalem's fall; how they cried, "Strip her, strip her to her very foundations!"

Psalm 137:8 Fair Babylon, you predator, a blessing on him who repays you in kind what you have inflicted on us;

Psalm 137:9 a blessing on him who seizes your babies and dashes them against the rocks!

Psalm 138:1 Of David. I praise You with all my heart, sing a hymn to You before the divine beings;

STEP TWO: Opening and Closing Markers

A thanksgiving conclusion appears in 136:26, while a hymnic opening appears in 138:1. A narrative opening separates 137:1 from the preceding thanksgiving, while a concluding curse separates it from Psalm 138. We do not have an occasion like Psalms 9 and 10 where an original psalm has been split in two by the copying and worship tradition, or Psalm 29 where two psalms of different content are merged into one.

STEP THREE: Translation Variances

Verse 1—Note translations that use present tense and those that use past, a difference in interpreting Hebrew verbal syntax.

Verse 2—Notice differing translations of names of trees and of instruments.

Verse 3—NLT interprets Zion as Jerusalem for ease of understanding.

Verse 4—NLT interprets strange or foreign land as pagan.

Verse 5—Note parentheses or other marks or notes as most translations add a line of explanation when Hebrew reads simply, "Let my right hand forget."

Verse 6—Note the expansion in the NET to read "give priority to."

STEP FOUR: Chronological Movement

Poetic pieces such as the Psalms can also include narrative elements with chronological movement. They can also include emotional movement from anger or frustration or mourning, to acceptance, to vow, to praise or thanksgiving. Psalm 137 includes both types of movement. Narrative movement occurs as the psalmist locates the Israelite group in exile in Babylon sitting and remembering their experiences in and allegiance to Zion or Jerusalem. They pick up their musical instruments and hang them on trees, it being no time for music. The Babylonian enemies enter the scene and mockingly demand examples of Israel's sacred music. The exiled Israelites ask a rhetorical question addressed to themselves rather than to the enemies, and expressing their hopeless situation void of mirth and joy. The psalmist suddenly changes the scene. The exiles address Jerusalem in the language of vow and self-curse. A further curse follows, directed this time to God and seeking harm on Edom, who helped Babylon destroy Jerusalem. The curse moves to quotation of Edom's words as they destroyed Jerusalem. The final curse turns to Babylon with horrendous words ironically expressed in the language of blessing. Thus the narrative movement here is that of imagined locale and of speakers, not of actual movement by characters.

Narrative movement is accompanied by emotional movement. Israelite weeping and mourning give way to Babylonian sarcasm and mocking. Israel responds in bewildered anger, seeing no reason to sing while in exile. This turns inward to a vow involving self-curse, a desperate form of pledging allegiance to homeland and not the "here land" of Babylon. Thoughts of homeland bring historical memories and historical hatred, first against Edom and then against Babylon, expressed in the most violent language imaginable. The many emotions expressed here all appear "negative" unless one sees the expression of national loyalty as positive despite its form of self-curse.

STEP FIVE: Genre or Type of Literature

Poetic parallelism normally marks Hebrew poetry. Thus two poetic lines either express the same thought in different words (synonymous parallelism) or express opposing thoughts (antithetical parallelism). Psalm 137 tends toward parallelism in some of its lines, especially verses 5–7, but the psalm is much more narrative-driven than poetic-style driven. Look rather at Psalm 138 to see synonymous parallelism. Psalm 37 combines synonymous and antithetic parallelism. For the latter see 37:9, 10–11, 12–13, 14–15, 17, 21, 22.

The question of genre here is complex. The opening verses (1–3) appear to introduce narrative. This gives a narrative tone to the remainder of the psalm, but many sub-genres appear. The first (3b) is the enemy's mocking song or taunt song requesting a song from Israelite exiles and thus arousing Israel's anger. Next is a rhetorical question addressed to no one in particular and expecting anyone hearing it to automatically supply the negative answer. A vow in the form of a self-curse (5–6) promises loyalty to Jerusalem and asks divine intervention in punishing the psalmist should devotion move from Jerusalem to Babylon. The curse expands to Edom, including a citation of Edom's response to Babylon's destruction of Jerusalem and an "eye for an eye" or "baby for a baby" judgment against Babylon.

Psalm 137 thus combines narrative, quotations of the enemy, taunt song, rhetorical question, self-curse, and curses against the enemies. The narrative remains unfinished, and the curses bring no divine action. Content and tone point to a community lament, but the normal lament genre elements (invocation, plea, complaint, affirmation of confidence) do not appear. The invocation of God's name comes only in verse 7 as part of a curse. The major plea comes in the form of a self-curse. The complaint appears only in the curse against the enemies, and the affirmation of confidence is vaguely implied by asking God to remember the enemies' evil actions. Psalm 137 thus demonstrates that a literary piece can function as a certain genre does without containing the normal elements of that genre.

STEP SIX: Key Teaching Verse(s)

Finding a key teaching verse here proves difficult. Verses 4–6 come closest with their call not to forget the joys of Jerusalem. Seen as a figure of speech here, Jerusalem represents God's dwelling place and the people's opportunity to meet God. This is the truth of the psalm's content, but that represents only one side of the psalmist's intent. The other side is the emotional climate of the psalm. This is a desperate prayer to God for deliverance and hope. The desperate hope from a desperate situation calls forth strong words of desperation. Prayer for one's own tongue to be silenced, for one's hand to wither, and for enemy babies' heads to hit the rocks is the strongest possible advocacy of violence. Yet the writer does not contemplate executing violence or involving his neighbors or armies in executing violence. Rather the psalmist seeks God and leaves the violent acts of retribution to the Deity alone. Poetic meaning thus comes from its use of imagery, its key content, and its emotional climate.

STEP SEVEN: Narrative Theme

Moving from rebellion against enemy demands to violent curse on the enemies, the psalm narrates the twin themes of loyalty to God and to the divine residence on earth and the call for retribution against the ruthless enemies. The intense nature of the narrative theme provides freedom for the congregation to pray in strong language in order to share with the Deity individuals' deepest desires, fears, and hopes. The psalm looses language for prayer that most people keep tightly bound, fearful of what God might think of such language. The psalmist says, speak from the depths. Don't worry about language. Rather, languish in the presence of God and in the certainty that God listens to whatever type of language you may use.

Example: Mark 8

STEP ONE: The Passage

New Revised Standard Version

Mark 8:21 Then he said to them, "Do you not yet understand?"

Mark 8:22 They came to Bethsaida. Some people brought a blind man to him and begged him to touch him.

Mark 8:23 He took the blind man by the hand and led him out of the village; and when he had put saliva on his eyes and laid his hands on him, he asked him, "Can you see anything?"

Mark 8:24 And the man looked up and said, "I can see people, but they look like trees, walking."

Mark 8:25 Then Jesus laid his hands on his eyes again; and he looked intently and his sight was restored, and he saw everything clearly.

Mark 8:26 Then he sent him away to his home, saying, "Do not even go into the village."

Mark 8:27 Jesus went on with his disciples to the villages of Caesarea Philippi;

Step TWO: Opening and Closing Markers

Let's look at just one part of this chapter, the verses above, for now. The rhetorical question of 8:21 closes the previous section. The change of location in 8:22 introduces the new passage. Sending the healed man home closes this section, while the change of location in 8:27 opens the next section. But Jesus' question in verse 21 follows from his charge of hardened hearts in verse 17 and calls attention to a larger scriptural unit. It points backwards into chapter 7 to the two cases of feeding the multitudes. It points forward to Peter's rebuke of Jesus in 8:32. This means a larger unit closes with the end of Jesus' speech in 9:1 and the temporal change in 9:2. The opening of this larger unit is more difficult to determine. It apparently goes back to 6:30 and the original feeding of the 5,000 (compare 6:52; 8:19). Sandwiched between the two feeding miracles are Jesus' walking on water (6:45–52), healing reports (6:53–56), the controversy with the Pharisees over eating bread and the disciples' lack of understanding (7:1–23), a Gentile woman willing to eat the bread crumbs of the dirty, despised dogs, the immediate healing of the deaf, speech-impaired man (7:31–37), Jesus' compassionate feeding of the 4,000 (8:1–10), the disciples' and the Pharisees' lack of understanding of the bread provisions (8:11–21). The larger section thus deals with provision of break and lack of understanding. The brief miracle of 8:22–26 stands in the theological center of the section, which then concludes with Peter's confession of Jesus as messiah (8:27–30), Jesus' first announcement of his coming death and resurrection leading to exchange of rebukes between Jesus and Peter (8:31–33), and Jesus' final call to loss of life for Jesus' sake (8:34—9:1).

STEP THREE: Translation Variances

The *New Living Translation* introduces "and heal him," providing what the Greek text implies but does not say.

NIV does not contain "to him," which NET and NLT clarify as "to Jesus."

Verse 24—NET gives a second meaning of the Greek verb, "regaining his sight." NLT interprets: "but I can't see them very clearly."

STEP FOUR: Chronological Movement

A. The Jesus party comes to Bethsaida, the home of Philip, Andrew, and Peter (John 1:44).

B. Friends bring blind man for Jesus to touch.

C. Jesus takes blind man by hand and issues him out of the city.

D. Jesus spits on man's eyes, lays hands on, and asks if man sees anything at all.

E. Blind man sees, but people appear as trees walking around.

F. Jesus places hands on man's eyes again, restoring full sight.

G. Jesus silenced man and sent him home with warning not to enter village.

The important note on the chronological narrative is the need for two tries before full healing occurs.

STEP FIVE: Genre or Type of Literature

The story is clearly a miracle story involving use of material substances, but becomes unique when a second try is needed.

STEP SIX: Key Teaching Verse(s)

Verse 25 is clearly the key verse in the story, describing Jesus' successful second effort, but for the larger unit, verse 24 comes up as the expected miracle succeeds only halfway so that men can be described as appearing to be something entirely different from the human race, namely trees.

STEP SEVEN: Narrative Theme

The narrative theme of the narrative itself is Jesus' persistent care until the man is healed and able to see. In the larger unit extending to 9:1, the emphasis turns to the unexpected "failure" of Jesus to heal the first time. He is about to give the key question to the disciples: Are they ready to take up a cross as Jesus must? Peter's rebuke of Jesus shows that even if the disciples know the proper language to use in describing Jesus, they still see only halfway, as did the blind man seeing men as trees walking. With this section the entire gospel of Mark turns direction, pointing to Jerusalem and the cross with the growing perception of the disciples' semi-blindness.

Now take a turn by examining the literary structure and meaning of Philippians 2.

STEP ONE: The Passage

STEP TWO: Opening and Closing Markers

STEP THREE: Translation Variances

STEP FOUR: Chronological Movement

STEP FIVE: Genre or Type of Literature

STEP SIX: Key Teaching Verse(s)

STEP SEVEN: Narrative Theme

Reflection Arising from Literary Study

1. In what way is masterful storytelling related to preservation of "historical facts"? Can facts be derived from a good story, or must we have strict, detailed battle reports?

2. What is the relationship of Joshua chapters 10, 11, and 12 to the literary art of chapter 2?

3. Does the conversation-dominated style of narrative writing in the Hebrew Bible necessarily report speech exactly as it was delivered on a historical moment? How does an author use such speeches to make a theological or moral point?

4. Are we supposed to read narrative literature as precisely chronological? Why or why not?

5. What style of writing best expresses deeply felt emotions? What limits does God or the Bible set on expressing such emotions to one another or to God?

6. In what way(s) does biblical narrative serve as a mirror for biblical characters and for us? Can stories involving other characters be intended to reflect our spiritual condition?

7. What meaning does one take from a passage that has meaning in itself and yet fuller and different meaning in the larger context, as in Mark 8?

CHAPTER 3: Exegetical

Historical

Theological

Devotional

Textual

Literary

Finding the Detailed Meaning

Exegetical Study

Details tell the story. Exegesis seeks to draw from the text the details of its vocabulary, grammar, syntax, and structure to determine the elements of meaning within the text and the central purpose of the entire passage within its context. Exegesis raises the following questions:

1. What important words does the writer use to make the point? Can you give a precise definition of words such as righteousness, justice, repent, mercy, Sheol? How can their occurrences elsewhere in the Bible help you refine your definition? What Bible tools will help you understand more clearly the meaning of these major biblical terms?

2. What grammatical, syntactical, or stylistic clues do you see in the passage? What is being affirmed? What is being contrasted? What is being denied? What is given for emotional effect rather than literal description? What is expressed as hyperbole or exaggeration? Is the speaker to be believed or doubted?

3. How does the writer relate to the audience? How is the audience supposed to react when hearing this Bible passage?

4. How does the writer relate to the main character of the narrative? Is the writer describing a hero or a villain?

5. What is the central purpose or point of the Bible passage you are studying? How does this tie in to the overall purpose of the particular Bible book you are studying?

We will use the passages of the previous chapter to seek answers to these questions: Joshua 2; Psalm 137; Mark 8; Philippians 2.

Example: Joshua 2

1. What important words appear?

Use a Bible Dictionary such as the *Holman Illustrated Bible Dictionary* (used below) or the *Harper's Bible Dictionary* or the *New Bible Dictionary* to discover the meanings.

A. Prostitute Rahab

"The most famous harlot in the Bible is Rahab of Jericho, who saved the Israelite spies sent by Joshua to scout out the promised land (Joshua 2). Israel spared her and her family when they conquered and destroyed Jericho. She continued to dwell with the Israelites (Joshua 6:23–25). She is listed in the genealogy of Jesus (Matthew 1:5). Her action on behalf of the Israelite spies won her a place in the roll call of the faithful (Hebrews 11:31; cp. James 2:25).

"The Bible gives few details of the ways in which harlots like Rahab practiced their trade. Evidently, harlots might solicit along the roadside (Genesis 38:14–15). Brothels, which often served as taverns and inns, were also known in the ancient Near East. Rahab's house may have been one (Joshua 2:1). It is possible that the prostitute had a distinctive mark on her forehead (Jeremiah 3:3) and breasts (Hosea 2:2). She might attract attention by her clothing, jewelry, and makeup (Jeremiah 4:30; Ezekiel 23:40; Revelation 17:4). Flattering with words (Proverbs 2:16) and making sweet music (Isaiah 23:16) might be used to lure or soothe a client. Her payment might be in money, or it could be in jewelry (Ezekiel 23:42) or other items of value (Genesis 38:15–18; cp. Luke 15:30).

"Although harlots were considered socially inferior, they did have legal rights, as is evident from the incident recorded in 1 Kings 3:16–22."

With the dictionary definition above, you can go to *Strong's Concordance*. Entries under *harlot, harlot's, harlots,* and *harlots'* will let you see all the passages where this word occurs and will show you the Strong key numbers that point you to the Hebrew and Greek sections at the back of *Strong's* to let you see all the passages with the same original language word. You can notice that the term clusters in Genesis 38; Joshua 2 and 6; and Ezekiel 16 and 23. Reading these passages will help you feel the emotional response Israelites had to harlots or prostitutes.

B. Given you the land

The only easy way to discover the meaning and occurrences of this phrase is to use a computer Bible study program, such as Accordance for

Macs, or the PC Study Bible or Quick Verse or many other fine programs for Windows. The program will show you that land occurs within five words of give in 104 verses. This is the central language of God's promises to Abraham and his descendants. See especially Genesis 12:7; 15:7, 18; 24:7; 35:12; 48:4; Exodus 6:4; 12:25; 13:5; Leviticus 14:34; 20:24; 23:10; 25:2, 38; Numbers 13:2; 14:8; 20:12, 24; 27:12; 32:5, 7, 9, 29; 33:53; Deuteronomy 1:35–36; 2:31; 3:18; 4:38; 5:31; 6:23; 8:10; 9:23; 19:8; 26:9, 15; 32:49, 52; Joshua 1:2, 13–14; 2:9, 14; 5:6; 9:24; 21:43; 23:16; 24:13; Judges 6:9; 18:10; 1 Kings 8:36; 9:7; 14:15; 2 Kings 21:8; 1 Chronicles 16:18; 2 Chronicles 6:27; 7:20; Nehemiah 9:8; Psalms 105:11; 135:12; 136:21; Jeremiah 3:18; 7:7; 11:5; 16:15; 24:10; 25:5; 30:3; 32:22; 35:15; Ezekiel 11:17; 20:15; 28:25; 33:24; 36:28; 37:25; 45:8; Amos 9:15.

C. Dread

Strong's will show you seventeen verses where the Hebrew word occurs, but you will soon note that translations give different English translations for the same Hebrew term: horror, fear, terror, dread, even idols. You can see the strength of this word the prostitute uses to describe the reaction of her people to Israel's coming in the power of their God.

D. Completely destroyed

Notice the *Strong's* definition of the Hebrew verb *charam*: "seclude; specifically (by a ban) to devote to religious uses (especially destruction); physical and reflexive, to be blunt as to the nose:—make accursed, consecrate, (utterly) destroy, devote, forfeit, have a flat nose, utterly (slay, make away)."

The term thus has a religious significance of making something accursed by devoting it to God by utterly destroying it. This is what God demanded Israel do to the Canaanite cities in the land God was giving them.

You can use the dictionaries and concordances to see the breadth of meaning and the importance of the following terms in this section.

E. Hearts melted

F. Courage failed

G. Your God is God

H. Show kindness

I. True sign

J. Our lives for yours

K. Built into the wall

L. Blood on his head

2. What grammatical or syntactical or stylistic clues do you find?

The phrase "especially Jericho" (v. 1) calls for attention, since the full sentence tells the spies to spy out the land as had the original spies in Numbers 13. "Especially Jericho" calls special attention to the city, prepares for the first battle in the promised land, and prepares for the actual narrative to follow in which Jericho is the only place visited. In verse 3, the king of Jericho will again emphasize, "the whole land."

Note the passive voice of verse 2, showing the message is important, not who delivered the message. Again in verse 9 the passive voice hides the messenger and emphasizes the message. An enemy prostitute repeats Israel's confession of faith.

The term "bedded down" or "laid down" is repeated in verses 1 and 8, showing what was expected in this institution.

The prostitute's story in verses 4–5 contradicts what she tells the men in verse 9. The repeated mention of the gate being shut shows the irony of the king's men being shut out and the Israelite spies being shut in.

Does verse 9 report a literal situation? Or does the prostitute use hyperbole or exaggeration to make her point? Note the figurative language of people melting.

Compare your translations of verse 12. Some begin with the oath formula, some with the immediate past action of grace and loyalty. Do you see a difference in meaning in the two sequences? The Hebrew first introduces the oath. This shows the prostitute's strength and control of the situation. She sees herself in position to demand something of the spies.

Verse 14 puts the power back in the hands of the spies as they make demands on the prostitute. Still the woman gets her way as the spies promise to treat her with the loyalty a covenant master expects from a slave.

Verse 16 shows the woman still in control directing the spies how to escape and save themselves. Use your math skills to determine how the "three days" statement (compare v. 22) fits into the rest of the chronology of Joshua 1—6. Note the men taking back the upper hand with the threat of verses 17–21.

The spies' report (v. 24) echoes the prostitute's report of rumors and reactions. They know about all the country from a brief bedding down in a prostitute's home. But the story is not complete. It foreshadows the action in the end of chapter 6. The prostitute's story thus forms a literary sandwich around the contents of crossing the Jordan, getting purified for battle, and conquering Jericho.

3. How does the writer relate to the audience? How is the audience supposed to react?

The writer apparently expects the audience to know the story and so tells it with an ironic twist, shifting the control of the story from prostitute to spies and back again. The audience should chuckle as they see the wily prostitute take charge and as they see spies get all the information they need for the entire country by a brief bedding down in a prostitute's place of business. Ultimately, the writer expects the audience to join the prostitute and spies in their confession of faith in the only God of heaven and earth.

4. Does the writer relate to the main character of the narrative as a hero or a villain?

The story opening leads us to look to the spies as the heroes, but quickly Rahab assumes that role. She makes the major speech. She leaves the spies dangling on a rope out of her window. She begins negotiations for the deliverance of her family. She fools the king's agents and directs the spies to safety. Thus the writer cleverly transposes a spy story into a prostitute's story. The prostitute becomes the amusing, ironic heroine whose position becomes clear only at the end of chapter 6.

5. What is the central purpose or point of the Bible passage?

The story itself illustrates the power of God to set the stage for the chosen people to take over the land. Even the enemy sees the inevitable when the God of heaven and earth acts. For later generations of readers already settled in the land, the story explains one reason why they have to live with foreigners in the land and assures them God is in control of life in the land, even life shared with foreigners. Israel's God remains God of both heaven and earth. This latter meaning becomes clear in the larger context when the final verses of chapter 6 complete the story. The larger context also shows how God prepared the way for the victory at Jericho.

Exercise: Psalm 137

You, the reader, can now work on understanding this brief psalm.

1. What important words appear?

2. What grammatical or syntactical or stylistic clues do you find?

3. How does the writer relate to the audience? How is the audience supposed to react?

4. Does the writer relate to the main character of the narrative as a hero or a villain?

5. What is the central purpose or point of the Bible passage?

Example: Mark 8:22–26

1. What important words appear?

A. Bethsaida

Strong's shows you Bethsaida was a small city in Galilee mentioned in Matthew 11:21; Mark 6:45; Luke 10:13; John 1:44; 12:21. John connects Philip, Nathanael, Peter, and Andrew with Bethsaida in Galilee. Jesus places a divine curse on the city for not responding to his miracles there (Mt. 11:20–24). *Eerdmans Dictionary* places it "3 km. (1.7 mi.) NNE of the mouth of the Jordan River on the Sea of Galilee."

B. Blind man

Strong's shows the New Testament replete with reference to the blind (Matthew 9:27–28; 11:5; 12:22; 15:14, 30–31; 20:30; 21:14; 23:16–17, 19, 24, 26; Mark 8:22–23; 10:46, 49, 51; Luke 4:18; 6:39; 7:21–22; 14:13, 21; 18:35; John 5:3; 9:1–2, 6, 8, 13, 17–20, 24–25, 32, 39–41; 10:21; 11:37; Acts 13:11; Romans 2:19; 2 Peter 1:9; Revelation 3:17). Blindness was connected to demon possession (Matthew 12:22). The blind often made a living by begging by the side of a road (Matthew 20:30; Mark 10:46; Luke 18:35; John 9:8). A popular view connected blindness with sin (John 9:2). Jesus wanted the blind invited to parties and banquets (Luke 14:13, 21). Divine punishment could cause blindness (Acts 13:11). Making the blind see was a convincing sign that Jesus was the Messiah (Matthew 11:5; 15:31; Luke 4:18; 7:22; John 9:32). Frequently, blindness is spiritual rather than physical, as many verses show.

C. Touch

"Touch" (Matthew 8:3, 15; 9:20–21, 29; 14:36; 17:7; 20:34; Mark 1:41; 3:10; 5:27–28, 30–31; 6:56; 7:33; 8:22; 10:13; Luke 5:13; 6:19; 7:14, 39; 8:44–47; 18:15; 22:51; John 20:17; 1 Corinthians 7:1; 2 Corinthians 6:17; Colossians 2:21; 1 John 5:18) appears most often in the gospels, frequently in connection with Jesus' miracles of healing. *Strong's* shows that the basic meaning is "to attach oneself to, i.e. to touch (in many implied relations)." It comes to denote simple touching so that the reader should not attempt to see a deep attachment of some kind in every reference to touch.

D. Spit

The specific Greek term used here appears only three times in the New Testament (Mark 7:33; 8:23; John 9:6), all in connection with healing. The *Holman Dictionary* hits another context of spitting by using Old Testament references: "Spitting at or on someone is the strongest sign of contempt. The brother who refused to perform levirate marriage (have a child by his brother's wife to carry on the name of the brother, Deuteronomy 25:5–6) would have his face spit in by the spurned wife of the brother (Deuteronomy 25:7–9). The soldiers that mocked Jesus before his crucifixion spat on him (Matthew 27:30). The religious leaders who tried Jesus before taking him to Pilate spat in his face (Matthew 26:67). Spittle was used to heal (Mark 8:23; John 9:6). Mixing spittle with clay (John 9:6) may have been to deliberately break the Sabbath laws of the Jewish religious leaders."

E. Restored

"Restored" (Matthew 12:13; 17:11; Mark 3:5; 8:25; 9:12; Luke 6:10; Acts 1:6; Hebrews 13:19) means "to reconstitute (in health, home or organization): restore (again)." The New Testament connects it with both physical healing (Matthew 12:13; Mark 3:5; 8:25; Luke 6:10) and end time renewal of the universe (Matthew 17:11; Mark 9:12; Acts 1:6). Again, just because the term can be used in an end time context does not give the interpreter the right to see an end time meaning in every context.

F. See clearly

"See clearly" appears twelve times in the New Testament (Matthew 6:26; 19:26; Mark 8:25; 10:21, 27; 14:67; Luke 20:17; 22:61; John 1:36, 42; Acts 1:11; 22:11). *Strong's* defines it as "to look on, i.e. (relatively) to observe fixedly, or (absolutely) to discern clearly: behold, gaze up, look upon, (could) see." This appears to mean more than just a glance. It is a centering of attention on someone with the intent to say something or do something in regards to the person. Yet, in itself, it has little theological content.

2. What grammatical or syntactical or stylistic clues do you find?

Who brought the blind man to Jesus? The antecedent for "they" is apparently the disciples, though Jesus is included in the previous collective subject. One could argue that people of the town brought the man to Jesus. Whoever brought him had confidence Jesus' touch would restore sight.

Jesus used two means of healing—spittle and touch. Jesus then, a bit shockingly, asked if the man saw anything. Why? Did Jesus not know? Did he want the crowd to hear the effect of the man's answer? Did he expect the answer to be negative? Was he not sure of his own healing ability?

The blind man offers an unexpected answer. Jesus' attempt to heal was not quite successful, the only such incident in the New Testament.

But the blind man saw something—trees! How did he know what trees looked like? Where did he get the poetic gift to create a figure of speech as strong as that of walking trees? Why did the second time work while the first did not? Why does the healed man not respond? The emphasis must be on the two stages of the healing, not on the man himself. Here the lesson is not whether the man expressed gratitude but on what it took to make the man see. Jesus was setting the stage for his next conversation with his disciples.

Recognize the textual problem at the end of verse 26. The Greek text makes a slight play on words. Jesus tells the man not to go *into* the village, and then Jesus, with his disciples, goes *out into* the village. Jesus wants at this stage to witness for himself, not have someone with only slight knowledge of him tell the world who he is. As the following passage will demonstrate, the disciples do not yet know who Jesus is.

3. How does the writer relate to the audience? How is the audience supposed to react?

The writer is setting the audience up. He leaves them in this story with more questions than answers. What is a healed man supposed to do if he cannot go visit his neighbors and share the news in town? Does healing bring only isolation? How can healing require two steps rather than one? Did Jesus fail the first time? Healing stories normally testify to the power of Jesus. Does this one have a different purpose? The audience is supposed to react with confusion and misunderstanding until they hear the next episode. At the beginning of this story, the disciples still did not understand (v. 21). At the end of the next episode Peter will be rebuking Jesus, and Jesus will be labeling Peter a Satan for not understanding the nature of Jesus' messiahship and not expecting suffering and death. The questioning reader must then ask how different he or she is from Peter. How willing are we to suffer and die for Jesus? Are we living "cross-ward"?

4. Does the writer relate to the main character of the narrative as a hero or a villain?

The main character is certainly Jesus, though the blind man shares center stage. The writer places the first shadow of doubt about Jesus in the readers' minds but has a purpose in doing so. One must see more than the all-triumphant Jesus. One must also see Jesus marching cross-ward to suffer and die for our sins. One must follow Jesus for more than healing and power. One must follow Jesus in humbling himself even to the death on the hated, shameful cross.

5. What is the central purpose or point of the Bible passage?

The passage turns the corner in Mark's gospel—from a healing Jesus gaining popularity and power to a Jesus walking to his God-given cross-shaped destiny. The two-step healing forces the reader to ask about who this Jesus really is, only to be confronted in the next passage with a Jesus whose eyes are on a cross, not a throne.

Now, it's again the reader's turn to deal with a passage.

Exercise: Philippians 2

1. What important words appear?

2. What grammatical or syntactical or stylistic clues do you find?

3. How does the writer relate to the audience? How is the audience supposed to react?

4. Does the writer relate to the main character of the narrative as a hero or a villain?

5. What is the central purpose or point of the Bible passage?

Reflection Arising from Exegetical Study

1. Every passage must be read in context. The passages that go before and those coming after tinge the passage under study with new light and new meaning.

2. No passage has meaning only in itself. Each passage plays a part in developing a bigger, stronger message for the reader.

3. Biblical writers generally have strong words they use to convey their message. The reader must use as many study tools as possible to find the particular meaning and message of a word in the present context. It is probably better to underplay the meaning of most words than to try to gain a secret, dominating meaning for the passage from one word.

4. The grammatical, syntactical, and stylistic structure of the passage must be determined if the reader wants to know the deepest meaning of the passage. These elements raise questions in the reader's minds and force a search for answers.

5. Most passages have an obvious hero or heroine. The writer's portrayal of this figure may well raise the most serious exegetical questions, leading to the key to the passage's meaning. The same hero figure may be treated differently at different places, as seen in the treatment of Peter in Mark 8 versus at Pentecost in Acts, or of Jesus in Mark 8:22–26 versus in the rest of the Gospel.

6. The aim of exegesis is to find the major point of a passage, not some minor detail that leads down a sermon or teaching path far

removed from the thought of the original author. The main point comes out of the study of the other exegetical and literary factors. The main point may be theological. For example, healing stories often point to the nature and power of Jesus. Parables often point to the nature of God's kingdom. Paul's letters often emphasize a major theological theme such as justification. The main point may be ethical. Much of the prophetic literature demands righteousness, justice, mercy, and loyalty. Jesus and Paul call for self-sacrifice, often expressed by Paul as being "in Christ." The major point may be assurance about end times as in Daniel and Revelation, but each of these begins with a strong ethical call that readers must not forget as they read the rest of the story. The major point may be one of praise and thanksgiving, or of confession and repentance, as seen in so many of the psalms and the openings of Paul's letters. Exegetical study leads one to find this major point amid all the details.

CHAPTER 4: Historical

Theological

Devotional

Textual

Literary

Exegetical

Finding What Happened

Historical Study

Have you ever given your class a pop quiz? A popular one is to list five to ten Bible events and ask members to put them in historical order. You might say:

1. Ezra

2. John the Baptist

3. Melchizedek

4. Noah

5. Elijah

6. David

7. Hezekiah

8. Paul

9. Samson

10. Adam

Historical study lets you be sure you can make a perfect score on such quizzes. But it does much more. Historical study lets you get to know Bible characters. It lets you fit each Bible section into the whole picture of God working with his people in and through history. It prepares you for questions that class members may innocently ask just because they have read the Bible and cannot put two of its pieces together into the proper historical framework.

Historical study lets you situate the Bible passage in the context of the larger world history of the times. Thus it reveals the tension and the decisions that biblical characters faced.

Historical study lets you find out where things took place and how the geography and topography of the land affected the situation. How hard was it to go down from Jerusalem to Jericho? How far out of the way did one go to avoid walking through Samaria? Where was the tribe of Dan living in the days of Samson? How far did Samson have to go to reach Philistine territory? Where is Mount Sinai? Why is it sometimes called Mount Horeb?

Historical study lets you see if the writer was an eyewitness to the events narrated or if some kind of oral or written sources supplied the information the inspired writer used.

Historical study lets you ask the question: Was telling a historical event the major purpose of the writer, or did the historical knowledge only serve as an example of a different kind of point the writer was making?

So how does one do historical study of the Bible? What questions do we ask? Where do we find answers? A good place to begin is geography. One must understand the diverse topography and climate of the very small land of Palestine.

Geography of Palestine

Setting
- Center of Fertile Crescent
- Between Mesopotamia (Assyria, Babylon, Sumer, Persia) on northeast and Egypt on southwest
- Vital for transport of international trade and military
- Confined by Mediterranean (the Great Sea) Sea on west and Arabian Desert on east

Size
- Coastline is 80 miles from Caesarea Maritima to Gaza
- Eastern length is 175 miles from Mount Lebanon to Dead Sea
- Northern width is 28 miles from Mediterranean to Sea of Galilee
- Southern width is 54 miles from Mediterranean Sea to Dead Sea

Geographical Features and Divisions
- Coastal Plain from Ladder of Tyre to Sinai Peninsula, interrupted by Mount Carmel but with few natural harbors and mainly sand dunes and limestone ridges to prevent coastland settlement; did have fertile soil and international highway

- Plain of Acco between Ladder of Tyre and Mount Carmel; controlled by Phoenician cities of Tyre and Sidon
- Sharon Plain from Mount Carmel to Yarkon River, marked by marshes and swamps with lush vegetation; Aphek was the most important city; in New Testament times Herod build important port of Caesarea Maratima.
- Plain of Dor between Carmel and Caesarea, often seen as part of Sharon Plain; dominated by port of Dor
- Plain of Philistia from Yarkon River down to Sinai; International Coastal Highway split in two directions here; Philistine cities of Gaza, Ashkelon, Ashdod, Gath, and Ekron dominated; no drainage problems; no large marshes and swamps; wonderful agricultural land

Jezreel Valley (Valley of Esdraelon)

- Runs northwest to southeast from Plain of Acco to Jordan Rift near Beth-shan. City of Jezreel separates eastern and western parts; important trade routes and cities of Megiddo, Yokneam, and Ibleam guarded passes through Mount Carmel; International Coastal Highway came through here from Megiddo; great grain crops; Kishon River in west and Jalud or Harod River in east

Western Mountains

- Hills 1500 to 4000 feet in height in Western Palestine, broken only by Jezreel Valley
- Galilee is north of Jezreel Valley; plateau in Upper Galilee with Mount Meron reaching 3963 feet; much forest land; isolated land; Lower Galilee had gentle hills and broad, fertile valleys with nothing over 2000 feet; vineyards, olive trees, wheat grown easily; towns of Nazareth, Cana, Sepphoris
- Samaria (Hill Country of Ephraim) south of Jezreel; mountainous country with numerous river valleys or wadis that are often dry but give up-and-down picture to the landscape; Ridge Road ran from Judea to Samaria near cities of Hebron, Bethlehem, Jerusalem, Bethel, Mizpah, Shiloh, and Shechem (between Mount Ebal and Mount Gerizim); western side of mountains well-watered; eastern side dry; highest point near Bethel is 3300 feet; Wadi Farah and Wadi Jabok link Samaria to Transjordan area of Gilead; good farmland, particularly in southern part
- Judah separated from Samaria by gentle depression called Saddle of Benjamin. Mountainous region between 2000 and 3400 feet; quite protected area; Wilderness of Judea to east is dry, rocky, desolate

going down 3500 feet from Jerusalem to Jericho; Negeb and desert areas to south and Shephelah to west; Terrace farming possible
- Shephelah is a strip of rolling foothills on western flank of Judah separating it from Philistine Plain; Judah and Philistia joined only by four wadis or valleys: Aijalon, Sorek, Elah, and Way to Hebron; vital military position with fortress towns of Lachish, Azekah, Socoh, and Timnah
- Negeb region surrounding Beersheba and Arad with ten to twelve inches of rain per year; in New Testament part of Idumea.

Southern Wilderness
- Almost rainless territory south of Beersheba; different parts called Wilderness of Zin and of Paran. Nabateans controlled in New Testament period and used irrigation to make the wilderness bloom; great peaks, depressions, and desolate plateaus mark the region.

Jordan Rift
- Reaches from eastern Turkey into Kenya; in Palestine is below sea level, with Dead Sea 1300 feet below sea level; between mountains on east and west
- Huleh Basin between Upper Galilee and Eastern Plateau marked on northeast by Mount Hermon (9,232 feet); springs here are sources of Jordan River; dangerous marshland promoting disease and hindering travel; good climate, water, and soil brought settlement of cities of Hazor, Dan, Abel-beth-maacah, and Ijon
- Sea of Galilee thirteen miles long and seven miles wide with surface 690 feet below sea level; also called Sea of Tiberias, Sea of Chinnereth, Lake Gennesaret, and the lake; northwest shore had International Coastal Highway and cities of Capernaum, Magdala, and Bethsaida; fishing and agricultural area
- Jordan Valley has 70-mile-long winding Jordan River; in north, key cities were Adam, Succoth, Zarethan, and Beth-shan; southern part is dry and desert-like as it comes to the Dead Sea

Dead Sea
- Dead Sea is 50 miles long and ten miles wide, with surface 1300 feet below sea level; this is lowest place on earth's land surface; Lisan Peninsula from east divides Dead Sea into two parts: northern part is 1300 feet deep, while southern part is 30 feet or less; extremely hot and dry; called Salt Sea and Sea of Arabah; Jordan supplies water from north and Arnon and Zered rivers enter from east, but waters have no exit

• Arabah south of Dead Sea 110 miles to Gulf of Aqabah; dry and desolate; rises to sea level about half way to Aqabah; had important copper mines and seaport of Ezion-Geber built by Solomon; important trade routes and so also military routes connecting to Arabia and Africa

Historical study requires a framework into which we can place all Bible events. The grid at the end of this chapter provides one such framework. Besides a geographical and chronological grid, historical study involves asking key questions, several of which are keyed closely to the literary questions. The basic historical study questions include:

1. What sources did the author have available?

   Are they poetry or prose?

   Oral or written?

   Eyewitness or secondary?

   Serious history or entertainment?

   Serious history or propaganda?

2. What major purpose did the author have?

   To write poetry or prose?

   To provide eyewitness or secondary accounts?

   To write serious history or entertainment?

   To write serious history or propaganda?

   To write serious history or theology?

   To serve historical purposes or worship purposes?

   Did the author also have a secondary purpose?

3. Does the writer prove to be at home in the historical, geographical, and cultural climates the material portrays, or does one find anachronisms, mislocations of sites, or different culture presuppositions from those of the time the writing describes? How are the chronological and geographical factors necessary for the story presented? Or could the story be told once upon a time from anywhere?

4. Does the author portray the characters realistically, or do they become stereotypes or bigger than life personalities?

5. Does the author's basic story line reflect the realities of history, or the plot lines of stories with narrative tension and resolution?

May the history writer borrow tools for the historian's craft from the narrative writer and still write history?

6. Does the historical narrative appear to be an isolated story, or is it fully incorporated into the rest of the narrative account? Must the reader know other parts of the story to understand this narrative?

7. What clues help you date the event? What clues point to the time of writing? How far removed in time and space may a writer be and still write accurate history?

8. What interpretation has the historian placed on the event? How can you tell?

9. What is the author's purpose in writing this narrative? Do you regard the writing as good history writing or not? Why?

Let us see how these questions relate to our chosen Bible passages.

Example: Joshua 2

1. What sources did the author have available?

Are they poetry or prose?
Prose narrative with some liturgical prose.

Oral or written?
The irony of setting—house of prostitution—and characterization—king's messengers outwitted by prostitute—apparently point to oral humor.

Eyewitness or secondary?
Oral roots of story may well reach back to eyewitness report, but this cannot be proven.

Serious history or entertainment?
Original oral version probably had high entertainment value. Preserved written form inserted into larger context converts it to historical purposes.

Serious history or propaganda?
Oral narrative obviously has propaganda purposes in showing Israel the weakness and foolishness of the Canaanite kings. It is placed in literary context for historical purposes.

2. What major purpose did the author have?

To write poetry or prose?
Prose but with emphasis on liturgical confession.

To provide eyewitness or secondary accounts?
To provide secondary report showing weakness of enemy and possibility of foreigners accepting Israel's God and thus becoming part of Israel.

To write serious history or entertainment?
Writer retains entertainment marks while writing history of faith by using familiar oral tradition.

To write serious history or propaganda?
Writer utilizes propaganda purposes to encourage armies, but has major purpose of teaching Israel its historical tradition with God, leading to chapter 24 and covenant renewal.

To write serious history or theology?
The writer's major purpose appears both in the central confession of faith by Rahab and in the narrator's final note in verse 24 about Yahweh giving the land. The historian writes history to teach theology.

To serve historical purposes or worship purposes?
Historian is working ahead to the speech of chapter 23 and the ritual of chapter 24 climaxing in the worship claim of 24:31. Thus history writing serves worship purposes.

Did the author also have a secondary purpose?
The writer wants Israel to learn history so they will become faithful followers and obedient servants of Yahweh rather than of Baal or other foreign gods.

3. Does the writer prove to be at home in the historical, geographical, and cultural climates the material portrays, or does one find anachronisms, mislocations of sites, or different culture presuppositions from those of the time the writing describes? How are the chronological and geographical factors necessary for the story? Or could the story be told once upon a time from anywhere?

Modern archaeologists raise strong questions about Jericho and the following story with Ai, not being able to find occupation layers and defense walls comparable to those of the story. A house built into a wall, an inn or house occupied by a prostitute(s), military spies, and the negotiation processes appear to fit the chronology. The internal chronology of the story presents some problems in correlating the three days of 1:11, 2:22; and 3:2. The geography fits the context of crossing the Jordan and setting up worship in Gilgal. The story could be told as a once upon a time event without specific location in time or space, but its literary setting gives theological motivation and impetus to the Israelite conquest.

4. Does the author portray the characters realistically, or do they become stereotypes or bigger than life personalities?

Only the prostitute gains any characterization in the story. The spies stereotypically follow first Joshua's and then Rahab's instructions. They briefly gain individuality as they turn Rahab's oath to their own advantage and place the initiative on her. Joshua plays a subordinate role in this narrative but is the only larger than life character in the larger narrative.

5. Does the author's basic story line reflect the realities of history, or the plot lines of stories with narrative tension and resolution? May the history writer borrow tools for the historian's craft from the narrative writer and still write history?

Quite obviously behind the current written version stands an oral tradition story with both a narrative line of tension/resolution and a comedic tension with Israelite spies bedded down in the place of business of a Canaanite prostitute. The narrative tension revolves around the need to hide spies from the royal messengers and then get the spies safely home. The resolution comes as the clever prostitute fends off these men's attempts to enter her establishment and then sends them off on a wild goose chase after spies still bedded down in the prostitute's bed. Certainly, a history writer can apply the narrative writer's craft to create comic relief, suspense, and tension into the historical record. History writing involves much more than compiling battle reports and lists. Human interest is in many ways the center of human history.

6. Does the historical narrative appear to be an isolated story, or is it fully incorporated into the rest of the narrative account? Must the reader know other parts of the story to understand this narrative?

The Rahab narrative can be easily isolated from the larger Joshua story, since Joshua appears only in the opening and closing scenes. The naming of Joshua is the connecting link to the larger narrative. To understand Rahab's confession of faith, the reader must be familiar with the even larger narrative of the exodus events.

7. What clues help you date the event? What clues point to the time of writing? How far removed in time and space may a writer be and still write accurate history?

The dating of the event rests with the larger issue of dating the exodus and conquest on the basis of 1 Kings 6:1, an issue too large for the current context. Many current scholars point to the writing as part of the so-called Deuteronomistic History under Josiah who died about 609 B.C.E.—or even later, in the exile. Did Israelite leaders really take materials with them that allowed them to record centuries of history so late? Or must we stay within the realms of the monarchy for source materials to be available to the writers? Whatever the dates of the event and of the writing, they are separated by several generations, even centuries. Current historians continue to write the histories of ancient civilizations like Rome, China, Mesopotamia, and Palestine. Possession of proper sources can enable a historian to write of times long gone by, especially in a civilization based on oral tradition and royal court annals.

8. What interpretation has the historian placed on the event? How can you tell?

As with every narrative, the narrator has omitted some of the facts. We do not know the spies' names. The details the narration does reveal are important, especially extended God-talk passages, repeated statements, and narrative-ending summary passages. This reveals the importance of Rahab's confession, the spies' promise of faithfulness, and the spies report to Joshua. Each of these key elements emphasizes one theme: God has given the land (vv. 9, 14, 24). The historian wants readers to join in the confession and see that they possess land as a divine gift, not as a human wage. Even foreigners join in the confession. This becomes the secondary theme of the narrative: the admission of faithful foreigners into the covenant community.

9. What is the author's purpose in writing this narrative? Do you regard the writing as good history writing or not? Why?

The writer has told a story in an interesting way that includes irony, humor, and emotional elements that maintain the readers' interest. At the same time, the historian has carefully tied the narrative back to the national foundation story of the exodus, to the unique claim that Yahweh is a unique God over all, and to the conquest under Joshua. The writer has used an interesting history lesson to teach basic theology to Israel. Thus the author has succeeded as a storyteller and as a historian. One's decision about the historical accuracy of all the details, especially the liturgical speeches, depends on one's view of Scripture and of the power of oral tradition to retain central historical elements as it preserves and repeats the narrative.

Example: Psalm 137

1. What sources did the author have available?

Are they poetry or prose?
The author has used historical tradition and presented it in poetic fashion, meaning that one must allow for poetic license, symbolism, and emotional overtones.

Oral or written?
The material is written in first person, so that the source is first generation oral tradition.

Eyewitness or secondary?
If one accepts the likely interpretation of poetic first person as true to life and not poetic license, then this is eyewitness testimony colored by first person emotional memory.

Serious history or entertainment?
The lament is anything but entertainment. It is a refusal to provide entertainment to cruel enemies. The history comes more in allusions than in straightforward history writing—Babylonian captivity of Judeans, Judean houses and apparently worship places near Babylon's rivers, memories of worship in Jerusalem at the temple, treachery by the Edomites during the sack of Jerusalem, recall of prophetic judgment oracles on Babylon.

Serious history or propaganda?
The psalm presents emotional history. This is not propaganda against an enemy so much as worshipers expressing their anger and grief before God and refusing to be interrupted by taunting enemies. The psalm presents loyalty and commitment to the ruined homeland and calls down divine curses on the horrific enemy. This shows the exiles' response to the dark side of history.

2. What major purpose did the author have?

To write poetry or prose?
To write emotion-laden poetry.

To provide eyewitness or secondary accounts?
To testify as an eyewitness and participant.

To write serious history or entertainment?
To write serious emotional history, not narrative history as much as the hurt and anger involved in responding to history.

To write serious history or propaganda?

The poet records the serious history of the worshipers in exile in a more personal history than a national history. In so writing, the psalmist may well seek others to join in the response.

To write serious history or theology?

Neither is uppermost in the psalmist's intention. The poet shows how theology works itself out in a local worship group following a national tragedy that brings personal consequences.

To serve historical purposes or worship purposes?

Psalm 137 is basically attuned to a lament service among the exiles. It expresses personal feeling more than theological or ethical teaching or reality. The psalmist will never take babies and throw their heads against the rocks, but deep down lies the desire to do so. Personal theology and ethics lead the psalmist to leave punishment and revenge to God no matter how strong the feelings may be. Thus the actions become part of lament and confession in worship, not actions on the streets of Babylon.

Did the author also have a secondary purpose?

The author may have wanted to show others the depth of feelings both in anger and in loyalty that overcame the exiles as they worshiped privately in Babylon. The author may have gone so far as hoping to evoke imitators who will join in such lamentation.

3. Does the writer prove to be at home in the historical, geographical, and cultural climates the material portrays, or does one find anachronisms, mislocations of sites, or different culture presuppositions from those of the time the writing describes? How are the chronological and geographical factors necessary for the story? Or could the story be told once upon a time from anywhere?

Exile's place was Babylon. Babylon and Edom were both involved in the destruction of Jerusalem. Babylon was part of the land between the rivers whose very existence depended on the rivers. Jews maintained their loyal worship while in exile. Some Jews settled permanently in Babylon as successful business people, but others maintained their loyalty to Jerusalem and the traditions of Yahweh. The emotions create a feeling of the exile culture. Thus the psalm appears to present authentic experiences historically, geographically, and culturally. This is not a once upon a time experience. It is an experience strongly rooted in the Jews' experience of Babylonian exile.

4. Does the author portray the characters realistically, or do they become stereotypes or bigger than life personalities?

The author presents self as one of the characters and shows self and fellow worshipers in a realistic, if possibly a bit overdrawn, poetic picture. Nothing is stereotypical about such strong emotional outbursts.

5. Does the author's basic story line reflect the realities of history, or the plot lines of stories with narrative tension and resolution? May the history writer borrow tools for the historian's craft from the narrative writer and still write history?

The poem does not develop a plot line. Rather it presents a series of vignettes picturing exile response. Here the poet has borrowed from the firsthand experience of history to develop an emotional portrait of exiles in torment.

6. Does the historical narrative appear to be an isolated story, or is it fully incorporated into the rest of the narrative account? Must the reader know other parts of the story to understand this narrative?

The poem represents part of an isolated worship experience among the exiles with no intention to be incorporated into any larger narrative. The poet sews isolated historical experiences together but not in a way to create historical narrative.

7. What clues help you date the event? What clues point to the time of writing? How far removed in time and space may a writer be and still write accurate history?

References to the Babylonian setting, vivid emotional reaction to the setting, memory of Edom's participation, and description of Jerusalem's loss all point to a date briefly after the Jews were taken into exile either in 597 or in 586 B.C.E. This writer shows how contemporary writers can preserve the strong emotions and reactions to a historical situation.

8. What interpretation has the historian placed on the event? How can you tell?

The poet has expressed the strongest of emotions to help fellow worshipers and, eventually, later readers experience the horror of exile and the strength of national loyalty. Self-curse, call for doom on Edom, a blessing on baby-killers all join to express and elicit the deepest and darkest feelings of the human heart. This is not an attempt to write history or teach history, but rather a call to emotional response to history.

9. What is the author's purpose in writing this narrative? Do you regard the writing as good history writing or not? Why?

The author provides an avenue of expression for discouraged, angry, ever-taunted and haunted exiles and for later readers and worshipers who face analogous situations that elicit similar feelings.

Example: Mark 8

1. What sources did the author have available?

Are they poetry or prose?
The writer has prose testimony to the events.

Oral or written?
Church tradition ties Mark closely to Peter. Both Matthew and Luke appear to depend on Mark's gospel. By definition, the so-called Q source excludes Mark, being the material common to only Matthew and Luke. Mark may have had written sources for his gospel, but much, if not all, his material came from oral testimony by Peter, according to church tradition.

Eyewitness or secondary?
If Peter is indeed the major source Mark used, then Mark had a major eyewitness source to the material he sets to writing, though the actual writer Mark was apparently too young to be a credible eyewitness.

Serious history or entertainment?
The gospel is good news about Jesus (1:1). It attempts to preserve for the church the story of Jesus. Mark can sprinkle in humorous, entertaining bits, as in Mark 14:51–52, but that is far from his purpose. He seeks to show the church the basic story of the Son of God whom they ignored or rejected or became confused about.

Serious history or propaganda?
In a sense, Mark presents propaganda against the Roman government and the Jewish leaders who combined in laying down the death sentence for Jesus. He shows the religious ineptitude of the scribes and Pharisees and the legal court ineptitude of Pilate. Still, that is merely a secondary motif in a book dedicated to preserve the church's memory of their Savior.

2. What major purpose did the author have?

To write poetry or prose?
Mark writes in Greek prose without poetic touches.

To provide eyewitness or secondary accounts?
Mark seeks to preserve and transmit in written form Peter's oral testimony about Jesus as well as various collections of Jesus tradition circulating among the churches.

To write serious history or entertainment?
See above.

To write serious history or propaganda?
See above.

To write serious history or theology?
Mark uses history to write theology. He portrays the person of Jesus and the demands of discipleship. He organizes the material in such a fashion that chapter 8 becomes the fulcrum of his gospel. Two bread miracles lead to an argument over bread, pointing to the disciples' inability to understand Jesus' mission. He warns disciples not to spread false teaching as the Pharisees do and not to follow the evil political maneuverings of Herod. A rhetorical question (v. 21) shows the disciples do not understand yet. The following miracle, with its unique two-stage healing process, points to the disciples' need for another stage of development as followers of Jesus. This stage gains relevance as Peter confesses Jesus as the Messiah, but Jesus does not yet let him tell that truth to others, because Peter has not learned the lesson of the suffering Messiah and the suffering followers, as shown by his rebuke of Jesus and Jesus' joining of Peter to Satan. This is historical narrative arranged and told to help uncertain, unsure disciples gain enough knowledge and courage and faith to follow Jesus cross-ward.

To serve historical purposes or worship purposes?
Mark's gospel may well have an intention behind it to provide the worshiping congregations material to read in their worship and learn the nature of messiahship and discipleship. That was only one intended use for a written testimony to preserve the church's traditions about its Lord as gradually church leaders and eyewitnesses began to die.

Did the author also have a secondary purpose?
See the immediately preceding question and answer.

3. Does the writer prove to be at home in the historical, geographical, and cultural climates the material portrays, or does one find anachronisms, mislocations of sites, or different culture presuppositions from those of the time the writing describes? How are the chronological and geographical factors necessary for the story? Or could the story be told once upon a time from anywhere?

This is a strongly debated issue about Mark's use of Galilean geography. He has to explain Aramean and Hebrew expressions to his audience. He has to explain Pharisaic rituals and customs. Mark may well be a Jerusalem resident who had not experienced northern Palestine. He does know Jewish customs and language, but his original readers are not expected to. Stories like the double-process healing or even the provision of bread could circulate as isolated narratives, but they have been carefully combined into a "good news of Jesus" narrative so that each element of the story plays a significant role in identifying messiahship and discipleship. Mark may well not place all materials in chronological order, but he takes accepted Jesus tradition and orders it for theological purposes.

4. Does the author portray the characters realistically or do they become stereotypes or bigger than life personalities?

Mark takes care to present characters around Jesus realistically and even negatively. They have strong traits and clearly defined weaknesses. They are not simply stereotypical followers. They are people torn between loyalty to this new master and concern at the direction the master seems to be taking them.

5. Does the author's basic story line reflect the realities of history, or the plot lines of stories with narrative tension and resolution? May the history writer borrow tools for the historian's craft from the narrative writer and still write history?

The basic plot line of the entire chapter artfully connects independent narratives about Jesus into a complex plot showing the disciples' struggles to understand and follow this beloved Master as he doggedly follows the path to the cross. The tension develops as Jesus keeps defining his role as one of suffering and martyrdom, while the disciples keep looking to the roles of procurator, king, and emperor. Mark has borrowed the narrative writer's skills and writing techniques to present the puzzle and mystery involved in identifying Jesus and defining discipleship.

6. Does the historical narrative appear to be an isolated story, or is it fully incorporated into the rest of the narrative account? Must the reader know other parts of the story to understand this narrative?

Mark has written a quite tight narrative. Study easily isolates separate traditions and narratives he has pulled out of tradition. Mark does not show us the actual chronology of Jesus' ministry so much as the ever-tightening danger Jesus faces as he determinedly walks toward the cross, inviting disciples to follow. One can understand some meaning from each of the separate narratives, but cannot understand Mark's true purpose without closely studying the entire book and its structure.

7. What clues help you date the event? What clues point to the time of writing? How far removed in time and space may a writer be and still write accurate history?

Chapter 8 is not a pointer to dating and chronology of the Jesus material. Most of the decisions on dating work on the basis of Mark 13 to find a date for the entire gospel around the Roman sack of Jerusalem in

70 C.E. This means the Jesus material had circulated in small clusters and collections for about forty years before being collected into a complete gospel. Even then, nothing of the birth and childhood years occurs, the good news beginning only with the ministry of John the Baptist. The widespread use of the Jesus traditions among the various churches set a standard as to the amount of variation permitted in relating the tradition. Mark thus collects and combines the various traditions into a complete story about Jesus showing who Jesus was and what Jesus expected a disciple to be.

8. What interpretation has the historian placed on the event? How can you tell?

The structure of Mark's gospel indicates the inadequacy of the disciples' statements about Jesus and expectations of Jesus. This shows how Mark has told the gospel to bring the church to a true understanding of who Jesus was, why he had to suffer, and what his suffering meant for the disciple life.

9. What is the author's purpose in writing this narrative? Do you regard the writing as good history writing or not? Why?

Mark writes to help the young church understand the sufferings and persecutions they were suffering as part of the expectations Jesus had for discipleship as he led the disciples to Jerusalem and the cross, answering their questions and rebuking their quarreling over position and power.

Exercise: Philippians 2
Reader's Time to Answer

1. What sources did the author have available?

Are they poetry or prose?

Oral or written?

Eyewitness or secondary?

Serious history or entertainment?

Serious history or propaganda?

2. What major purpose did the author have?

To write poetry or prose?

To provide eyewitness or secondary accounts?

To write serious history or entertainment?

To write serious history or propaganda?

To write serious history or theology?

To serve historical purposes or worship purposes?

Did the author also have a secondary purpose?

3. Does the writer prove to be at home in the historical, geographical, and cultural climates the material portrays, or does one find anachronisms, mislocations of sites, or different culture presuppositions from those of the time the writing describes? How are the chronological and geographical factors necessary for the story? Or could the story be told once upon a time from anywhere?

4. Does the author portray the characters realistically, or do they become stereotypes or bigger than life personalities?

5. Does the author's basic story line reflect the realities of history, or the plot lines of stories with narrative tension and resolution? May the history writer borrow tools for the historian's craft from the narrative writer and still write history?

6. Does the historical narrative appear to be an isolated story, or is it fully incorporated into the rest of the narrative account? Must the reader know other parts of the story to understand this narrative?

7. What clues help you date the event? What clues point to the time of writing? How far removed in time and space may a writer be and still write accurate history?

8. What interpretation has the historian placed on the event? How can you tell?

9. What is the author's purpose in writing this narrative? Do you regard the writing as good history writing or not? Why?

One Approach to Biblical Chronology

Do not let the length of the grid scare you away. You are not asked to memorize the grid, just to have it handy when you are doing Bible study. Look at the grid for a few moments to see the type of information available in it. Then read on to see how little of the grid you really need to know.

EVENT	LOW CHRONOLOGY	HIGH CHRONOLOGY
Abraham	1900	2100
Joseph in Egypt	1700	1900
Exodus	1250	1440
Joshua/Conquest of Canaan	1200	1400
Judges	1150–1000	1370–1000
KING	**JUDAH/PROPHET**	**ISRAEL/PROPHET**
Saul	1020–1000	1020–1000
David	1000–960	1000–960
Solomon	960–922	960–922
Rehoboam	924–907	
Jeroboam I		924–903
Abijam	907–906	
Asa	905–874	
Nadab		903–902
Baasha		902–886
Elah		886–885
Omri		885–873
Jehoshaphat	874–850	
Ahab		873–851/Elijah
Ahaziah		851–849
Jehoram	850–843	
Jehoram		849–843/Elisha
Ahaziah	843	
(Athaliah)	843–837	
Jehu		843–816
Joash	800–783	
Jehoahaz		816–800
Jehoash (Joash)		800–785
Jeroboam II		785–745/Amos
Uzziah (Azariah)	783–742/Isaiah	

KING	JUDAH/PROPHET	ISRAEL/PROPHET
Zechariah		745
Shallum		745
Menahem		745–736
Jotham	742–740/Isaiah	
Ahaz	742–727/Isaiah	
Pekiah		736–735
Pekah		735–732
Hoshea		732–723
Hezekiah	727–698/Isaiah, Micah	
EVENT	**JUDAH**	**NEAR EAST**
Fall of North/Samaria to Assyria		722/Sargon II of Assyria 722–705
Siege of Jerusalem		701/Sennacherib of Assyria 705–681
Manasseh	697–642	Esarhaddon of Assyria 681–669
Amon	642–640	Ashurbanipal II of Assyria 669–627
Josiah	639–609	Nabopolassar of Babylon, 626–605
Nineveh destroyed, 612		
Jehoahaz	609	
Jehoiakim	608–598/Jeremiah, Obadiah	Nebuchadnezzar of Babylon, 605–562;
		Battle of Carchemish, 605
Jehoiachin	598–597	First campaign against Judah, 598
Zedekiah	597–586/Jeremiah, Ezekiel	
Babylon Destroys Jerusalem	586	
JUDEA	**PERSIA**	**BABYLON**
		Evil-Merodach of Babylon, 562–560
Jehoiachin freed from Babylonian prison, 2 Kg 25:27–30		
First return to Jerusalem from Exile, 538; Ezra 1:1–4; 6:13–15	Cyrus II the Great 559–530, captured Media, 550; Lydia, 546; and Babylon, 539; let Jews return to Jerusalem, 538; see Isa 45:1	Neriglissar of Babylon, 560–556; see Jer 39:3

JUDEA	PERSIA	BABYLON
		Labash-marduk, 556
		Nabonidus, 556–539
		Belshazzar, regent for Nabonidus, who was out of country on archaeological digs
	Cambysses II 530–522; conquered Egypt, 525	
Haggai and Zechariah preached, 520; temple rebuilt and dedicated, 515	Darius I, 522–486; invaded Greece; defeated at Marathon, 490	
Book of Esther	Xerxes I, 486–465; sacked Athens, 480; defeated in naval battle of Salamis, 480	
Ezra leads group to Judah, 458		
Nehemiah leads group to Judah to rebuild walls, 444	Artaxerxes I 465–425; peace of Callias with Greece, 449	

JUDEA	PERSIA	GREECE
	Xerxes II 423	
Jews in Elephantine in Egypt ask Jerusalem for help in rebuilding temple in Egypt, 407	Darius II 423–404	Peloponnesian War, 431–404; Persian gains Greek cities in Asia Minor
	Artaxerxes II 404–359; lost Egypt and had other satraps revolt	
	Artaxerxes III 359–338; regains Egypt, 342	Philip II of Macedon gains power; Alexander the Great born, 356
	Arses 338–336	
	Darius III 336–330	Philip assassinated 336; Alexander invades Persia, 334; Darius defeated at Issus, 333; Alexander gains Egypt and Palestine, 332–331; moves clear to India by 323, but died in Babylon, 323

JUDAH	PTOLEMIES OF EGYPT	SELEUCIDS OF SYRIA
Many Jews settled in Egypt	Ptolemy I Soter 323–285	Seleucid I 312–280; Antioch founded
Septuagint (LXX) begun in Alexandria	Ptolemy II Piladelphus 285–246; first and second wars with Seleucids	Antiochus I, 280–261
		Antiochus II 261–246

JUDAH	PTOLEMIES OF EGYPT	SELEUCIDS OF SYRIA
	Ptolemy III Euregetes 246–221	
	Third war with Seleucids	Seleucus II 246–223
	Ptolemy IV Philopator 221–203; defeated Antiochus III at Raphia	Antiochus III 223–187; gained rule over Palestine at Pnias, 200; defeated by Trajan/Rome in Asia Minor at Magnesia, 190
Heliodorus of Syria tries to plunder temple in Jerusalem	Ptolemy V Epiphanes, 203–181	Seleucus IV 187–175
Antiochus bought high priesthood in Jerusalem; invaded Egypt until Romans forced withdrawal; had pig offered on altar in Jerusalem; provoked Maccabean revolt	Ptolemy VI Philometor, 181–146	Antiochus IV Epiphanes 175–163

DATE	MACCABEAN LEADER	EVENTS
167–166	Mattathias	Refused to sacrifice to Antiochus IV
166–160	Judas Maccabeus	Led revolt against Seleucids; won military victories; cleansed temple in 164 B.C.; gained religious freedom for Jews in 162; died in battle
160–142	Jonathan	Continued guerilla warfare from Michmash; appointed High Priest in 152; executed by the Seleucid Trypho in 143
142–134	Simon	Got concessions from Seleucids creating independent Jewish state; 142 B.C.

DATE	HASMONEAN RULERS	EVENTS
135–104	John Hyrcanus, last of Maccabean brothers	Conquered Medeba, Idumea, Samaria, and Joppa; Pharisees and Sadducees appear at this time
104–103	Aristobulus	Killed all but one of his brothers, sons of Hyrcanus; conquered upper Galilee; used title King
103–76	Alexander Jannaeus	Gained Gaza, Dora, Anthedon, Raphia, Strato's Tower; parts of Transjordan; civil war against Pharisees
76–67	Salome Alexandra, Alexander's widow	Favored Pharisees; made son Hyrcanus II the high priest

DATE	HASMONEAN RULERS	EVENTS
67–63	Hyrcanus II and Aristobulus II, brothers	Sadducees supported Aristobulus and gained power; Idumean governor Herod Antipater supported Hyrcanus; Pompey of Rome took over control in 63 B.C.E.

DATES	LEADERS OF ROME	EVENTS IN ROMAN HISTORY
1000 B.C.E.		Traditional settlement of Rome
753	7 kings found Rome as political power	
509		Expulsion of Etruscan rule; establishment of Roman Republic
390		Gauls sack Rome
312		Construction of Via Appia, first great Roman road
264–238		Roman conquest of Italian peninsula; First Punic War with Carthage; annexation of Sicily, Sardinia, Corsica

DATES	LEADERS OF ROME	EVENTS IN ROMAN HISTORY
218–202		Second Punic War; Hannibal campaigns in Italy; Carthage defeated; Spain occupied; First Macedonian War (214–205)
200–197		Second Macedonian War; Philip V defeated; Rome invades Asia and defeats Antiochus III at Magnesia, 190
171–168		Third Macedonian War
150–148		Fourth Macedonian War; Macedonia annexed as province
146		Corinth destroyed; Third Punic War (149–146); Carthage destroyed; Africa annexed as province
133		Attalus III wills Attalid kingdom centered in Pergamum to Rome
112–105		First war with Jugurtha, king of Numidia; revolt against the Senate

DATES	LEADERS OF ROME	EVENTS IN ROMAN HISTORY
88–84		War with Mithradates of Pontus
74		Annexation of Bithynia and Cyrene
73–71		Slave revolt of Spartacus
66–63	Pompey	Conquers Syria and Palestine
60	First Triumvirate—Julius Caesar, Pompey, Crassus	
58–51	Julius Caesar	Conquers Gaul
49–45	Pompey and Caesar civil war	
48	Pompey dies	
46	Julius Caesar becomes dictator of Rome	
44, March 15	Senators murder Caesar	
42	Mark Antony and Octavian defeat Caesar's assassins at Battle of Philippi	
42–31	Octavian in west and Antony with Cleopatra in east fight	
31	Octavian defeats Antony and Cleopatra at Actium in Greece	
27	Octavian entitled Augustus; Roman Empire begins	
DATES	LEADERS OF ROME	NEW TESTAMENT EVENTS
27 B.C.E..– 14 C.E.	Caesar Augustus (Octavian)	Birth of Jesus; death of Herod (4 B.C.E.); in 6 C.E. procurators named in Judea
14–37 C.E.	Tiberius	Public ministry of Jesus about 24 C.E. to 27 or 26 to 30; Pentecost; Paul's conversion
37–41	Gaius (Caligula)	Kingdom of Herod Agrippa I (41–44)
41–54	Claudius	Martyrdom of James; James written; Paul's first missionary journey (46–48); Jerusalem Conference (49); Jews expelled from Rome (Acts 18:1); Second Missionary Journey (50–52); Zealot riots; early Pauline letters (Thessalonians, Galatians; Corinthians; Romans

DATES	LEADERS OF ROME	NEW TESTAMENT EVENTS
54–68	Nero	Third Missionary Journey (53–57); Paul imprisoned at Caesarea (57–59); Paul's voyage to Rome and prison there (60–62); prison letters written (Ephesians, Colossians, Philemon, Philippians); Jude written; great fire Nero set in Rome (64); Jewish persecution; Jewish revolt (66); Paul's second Roman imprisonment (?) (66–67); pastoral letters written (Titus, Timothy) martyrdom of Paul and Peter; Gospel of Mark written; letters of Peter written
68–69	Four Emperors: Galba, Otho, Vitellius, Vespasian	
69–79	Vespasian	Titus besieges and destroys Jerusalem (70); Masada falls (73–74); Gospel of Matthew and Luke/Acts written (?)
79–81	Titus	Rome burns
81–96	Domitian	Dacian Wars 86–87,89,92; Christians persecuted; Hebrews, letters of John, Gospel of John, Revelation written
DATES	LEADERS OF ROME	EARLY CHURCH EVENTS
96–98	Nerva	
98–117	Trajan	Nabatea annexed; Christians persecuted in the east; Parthian wars and conquests (114–117); second Jewish revolt (115–117)
117–138	Hadrian	Bar Kokhbah rebellion in Palestine (132–135); Jerusalem rebuilt as Roman Colony

Dates to Remember

The grid takes you from Abraham all the way to one hundred years after Christ's death. The time span reaches from Genesis 12 to a time span over sixty years beyond the Book of Acts and about forty years after John wrote Revelation on the island of Patmos. We can round a few of these dates off to make the following chart easy to memorize so that you will have a basic framework into which you can plug any biblical event to which you find reference. These dates you should be able to quote to anyone who asks for such information. Note that you may not want to memorize the international events. We provide them for a broader context.

DATE	ISRAELITE EVENT	MAIN PERSON(S)	INTERNATIONAL EVENT
2000	Call of Abraham	Abraham	Hammurabi of Babylon about 1800
1000	Israelite monarchy begins	David	Iron Age; Rise of Assyria under Tiglath-pileser I about 1100
900	Israelite monarchy splits	Rehoboam and Jeroboam I	Shishak (Sheshonk) of Egypt invades Judah (1 Kings 11:40; 14:25–26)
722/21	Fall of Northern Kingdom to Assyria	Sargon and Sennacherib of Assyria	Assyrian Empire
586	Destruction of Jerusalem by Babylon/exile begins	Nebuchadnezzar of Babylon	Battle of Carchemish 605; fall of Assyria
538	First return from exile	Sheshbazzar (Ezra 1)	Cyrus of Persia defeats Babylon (539)
515	Second temple dedicated	Zerubbabel, Haggai, Zechariah	Cambysses of Persia defeats Egypt (525); Darius of Persia defeated by Greeks at Marathon
458/444	Ezra brings law, Nehemiah leads building of walls in Jerusalem	Ezra, Nehemiah	Artaxerxes of Persia; peace of Callias with Greece in 449
332	Palestine falls to Alexander	Alexander the Great	Death of Alexander in Babylon 323; Ptolemies in Egypt and Seleucids in Syria contend for Palestine
167	Antiochus Epiphanes of Syria desecrates temple with pig sacrifice	Antiochus, Mattathias	
162	Jews win religious freedom	Judas Maccabeus	
142	Independent Jewish State—Maccabean rulers; then Hasmoneans	Simon Maccabeus	

DATE	ISRAELITE EVENT	MAIN PERSON(S)	INTERNATIONAL EVENT
63	Romans take control		Pompey is Roman general
6 B.C.E.	Birth of Jesus	Mary, Joseph, Jesus	Herod the Great rules (37 to 4 B.C.E.) for Rome and Caesar Augustus
27 C.E.	Crucifixion	Jesus, John, Mary	
28–29 (?) 32	Paul's conversion	Paul	
43/44 (??) or 49	Jerusalem Conference	Paul, Peter, James	
64 (?)	Paul martyred	Paul, Nero	Nero burns Rome
70	Titus destroys Jerusalem	Titus the Roman general	

The Herod Family

You will want several other historical facts at hand as you do historical study, especially as you study the New Testament. First is a differentiation between the several "Herods" mentioned.

1. Herod the Great, king of Judea; cruel, ruthless, despised; rebuilt temple; other massive building projects; when Jesus was born, this Herod had babies slaughtered

2. Herod Archelaus, Ethnarch of Judea, Samaria, and Idumea; brutal, oppressive; led to Mary and Joseph settling in Nazareth rather than Judea; removed from office by Augustus, and replaced by procurators; son of Herod the Great

3. Philip, tetrarch to the north and east of Sea of Galilee; had capital at Caesarea Philippi; another son of Herod the Great

4. Herod Antipas, tetrarch of Galilee and Perea, ruled during Jesus' ministry in Galilee; Jesus called him a "fox"; participated in part of final trial of Jesus; John's condemnation of his adulterous marriage led to his ordering the execution of John the Baptist; he was defeated by Artas IV, King of Nabateans; rebuilt Sepphoris; built Tiberias on Sea of Galilee; deposed by Caligula; also son of Herod the Great

5. Herod Agrippa I, King of Judea; grandson of Herod the Great.

6. Herod Agrippa II, tetrarch and King Chalcis; son of Herod Agrippa I.

The Herods and the Bible

RULER	FAMILY RELATION	TERRITORY	DATES RULED	BIBLE REFERENCE
Antipater II	Son of Herod Antipater I	Idumea and Judea	Ca. 50–43 B.C.E.	
Herod the Great	Son of Herod Antipater II	King of Judea	37–4 B.C.E.	Matthew 2:1–22; Luke 1:5
Herod Archelaus	Oldest son of Herod the Great	Ethnarch of Judea, Samaria, and Idumea	4 B.C.E.–6 C.E.	Matthew 2:22
Philip	Son of Herod the Great and Cleopatra of Jerusalem	Tetrarch of territories north and east of the Sea of Galilee, centered in Caesarea Philippi	4 B.C.E.–34 C.E.	Luke 3:1
Herod Antipas	Youngest son of Herod the Great; second husband of Herodias, formerly married to Philip and mother of Salome	Tetrarch of Galilee and Perea	4 B.C.E.– 39 C.E.	Matthew 14:1–11; Mark 6:14–29; Luke 3:1,19; 13:31–33; 23:7–12
Herod Agrippa I	Grandson of Herod the Great	King of Judea	37–44	Acts 12
Herod Agrippa II	Son of Herod Agrippa I and sister of Bernice, with whom he had close relationships	Tetrarch and King of Chalcis and then heir to Philip's territory plus parts of Galilee and Perea	44–100	Acts 25:13—26:32

Procurators over Judea and Samaria after Herod Archelaus

1. Coponius   6–9 C.E.

2. Ambibulus   9–12

3. Annius Rufus   12–15

4. Valerius Gratus 15–26

5. Pontius Pilate   26–36

(Pilate ruled Judea during Jesus' ministry, dealt harshly with Jews, presided at Jesus' trial, ruled during Day of Pentecost and birth of church, and was removed from office by Syrian Legate Vitellius.)

6.	Marcellus	37
7.	Marullus	37–41

Jesus and His Ministry

To do historical study, you will want some background material on Jesus and his ministry.

Presence of Jesus the Messiah on Earth (4) 6 b.c.e.– 27 (30) c.e.

A. Jewish Religious Groups the Messiah Encountered

1. Pharisees
   a. Probably arose in Maccabean Period
   b. Lay movement dedicated to observing Jewish law and interpreting rules for how law applied in their day
   c. Closely related to the scribes, the official interpreters of the law.
   d. Theological moderates balancing divine sovereignty and human freedom; believed in angels, demons, heaven and hell, resurrection
   e. Scrupulously practiced written and oral law
   f. Included Hillel, Shammai, and Gamaliel—Paul's teacher
   g. Jesus debated with them over their oral law and their motives
   h. Survived destruction of temple in 70 c.e., producing rabbinic Judaism with its literature—Mishnah, Gemara, Talmud

2. Sadducees
   a. Arose under the Maccabeans
   b. Represented aristocrats and social leaders of Judaism, including the priests
   c. Centered in temple; dominated Sanhedrin
   d. Led opposition to Peter and John in Acts 4 — 5
   e. Cooperated with Roman rulers pragmatically and adopted Hellenistic culture
   f. Rejected all authoritative writings and teachings except for Genesis-Deuteronomy; denied eternal rewards and punishment, resurrection, angels and demons.
   g. Vanished after fall of Jerusalem in 70 c.e.

3. Essenes and Dead Sea Scroll Community

    a. Essenes lived in various towns throughout Judea; Dead Sea Scrolls group lived from 150 B.C.E. to 68 C.E. near Qumran at northern end of Dead Sea

    b. Withdrawn covenant community opposing Jerusalem religion

    c. Emphasized study of Scripture and ritual purification

    d. Expected divine intervention in world in near future with prophet and two messiahs—one priestly, and one Davidic

    e. Followed teachings of a leader called "Teacher of Righteousness"

    f. Led by supreme council; had extremely strict discipline

    g. Excavations around Qumran uncovered earliest known biblical scrolls, produced by this group

4. Zealots

    Little known group who opposed Roman government radically and sought to reestablish Davidic monarchy

B. Life of Jesus the Messiah

    1. Birth 6 B.C.E.

    2. Flight to Egypt 4 B.C.E.

    3. Teaching with Religious Leaders in Temple 6 C.E.

    4. Working as Carpenter in Nazareth

    5. Ministry of John the Baptist Begins

    6. Baptism of Jesus

    7. Calling of First Disciples

    8. First Passover During Jesus' Ministry

    9. Events of John 3 — 4, ministry in Galilee

    10. Feast of Tabernacles (John 5:1)

    11. Ministry in Galilee

    12. Passover Feeding of 5,000

    13. Final Ministry in Galilee, Withdrawal, Return

    14. Feast of Tabernacles (John 7:1—10:21)

    15. Return to Galilee and Perean Ministry

    16. Final Trip to Jerusalem

    17. Hanukkah in Jerusalem (John 10:22)

    18. Judean Ministry

19. Triumphal Entry, Passion Week
20. Crucifixion and Resurrection

C. Structure of Jesus' Ministry According to the Gospels

  1. Matthew's Gospel, Built around Five Sermons
    a. Infancy 1 — 2
    b. Sermon on the Mount 5 — 7
    c. Miracles and Calling of Disciples 8—9
    d. Sermon Sending Disciples on Mission 10
    e. John's Questions and Pharisees Arguments 11—12
    f. Sermon of Parables by the Sea 13
    g. Healings, Feedings, Disputes, Looking to Cross 14—16
    h. Transfigurationch 17
    i. Sermon on Humility 18
    j. Teachings Approaching Jerusalem 19— 22
    k. Sermon on Final Coming of the Kingdom 23— 25
    1. Arrest, Trial, and Crucifixion of Jesus 26— 27
    m. Resurrection and Commission of Jesus 28

  2. Mark's Gospel, Built around Passion Predictions and Disciple's Reactions
    a. Jesus' Ministry Choosing and Preparing Disciples 1:1— 8:30
    b. Jesus' Passion Predictions, Calls to Discipleship, Passion, and Resurrection 8:31—16:8

  3. Luke's Gospel, Built around Revealing Who Jesus Is
    a. Infancy, Preparation by John, Baptism, Genealogy, and Temptation 1:1—4:13
    b. Galilean Ministry of Authoritative Savior Revealing Divine Glory 4:14—9:50
    c. Journey to Jerusalem Revealing Savior's Mission and Disciples' Mission 9:51—19:44
    d. The Savior's Atonement for the World's Sin 19:45—23:56
    e. The Savior's Triumph in Resurrection and Ascension 24:1–53

  4. John's Gospel, Built around Seven Signs and Discourses Leading to the Savior's Passion

      a. Introductory Testimony to Eternal Word　1

      b. Jesus and Jewish Institutions: Changing Water to Wine, Cleansing the Temple, and Healing at a Distance 2:1—4:54

      c. Jesus and the Jewish Festivals: Healing Impotent Man, Feeding Five Thousand, Healing Man Born Blind 5:1—10:21

      d. Jesus as the Resurrection and the Life: Raising of Lazarus 11:1–57

      e. Preparing for Death in Teaching and Action　12:1—17:26

      f. Arrest, Trial, and Crucifixion　18:1—19:42

      g. The Resurrection　20:1–29

      h. Concluding Purpose and Testimony　20:30—21:5

D. The Infancy of Jesus

    1. Presented as the Eternal Word

    2. Birth of John the Baptist Predicted

    3. Birth of Jesus Predicted

    4. Born of Davidic Line

    5. Conceived of a Virgin

    6. Mothers of John and Jesus Meet

    7. Birth of John the Baptist

    8. Born in Bethlehem

    9. Visited by Shepherds

   10. Circumcised with Testimony of Simeon and Anna

   11. Visited by Wise Men

   12. Flight to Egypt

   13. Slaughter of Infants by Herod

   14. Called Out of Egypt to Nazareth

   15. Grew in Spirit, Wisdom, Grace of God, and Size

   16. Discussing with Jewish Religious Leaders in Temple

E. Jesus' Final Week

    1. Anointing in Bethany—Saturday

    2. Triumphal Entry—Sunday

    3. Temple Cleansing and Curse of Fig Tree—Monday

    4. Teaching in Temple and on Mount of Olives—Tuesday

    5. Unknown—Wednesday

    6. Preparation for Passover, Last Supper, Gethsemane, Arrest—Thursday

    7. Trials, Sentence, Execution, Burial—Friday

    8. In Grave—Saturday

    9. Resurrection—Sunday

F.   Jesus' Final Hours

    1. Thursday after Sundown: Last Supper, Prayer in Garden, Betrayal and Arrest

    2. Night of Thursday-Friday: Custody, Hearing before Annas, Trial before Caiaphas, Peter's Denial

    3. Friday Morning Early: Sanhedrin Completes Deliberations, Jesus Sent to Pilate, Hearing Before Pilate, Jesus Sent to Herod, Jesus Returned to Pilate

    4. Friday around Noon: Jesus Nailed to the Cross

    5. Friday Midafternoon: Jesus Dies

    6. Friday Near Sundown: Jesus Buried

Paul's Ministry

    Another set of facts centers on Paul's ministry and very approximate dates within it.

Approximate Calendar of Paul's Life*

DATES	EVENT
32	Conversion
35	First Jerusalem visit after conversion (Gal. 1:18–19)
35–43	Silent Years in Syria and Cilicia (Gal. 1:21)
43–44	Ministry with Barnabas in Antioch (Acts 11:26)
44	Death of Herod Agrippa I
45/46	Famine Visit to Jerusalem (Acts 12:25)
45/46–47/48	First Missionary Journey (Acts 13—14)
48	Return to Antioch
48	Jerusalem Conference (Acts 15; Gal. 2)
48–52	Second Missionary Journey (Acts 15:36—18:17)
48–49	Antioch to Troas (Acts 15:36—17:15)

49–51	Macedonia and Athens (Acts 17:16–34)
51–52	Corinth (Acts 18:1–17)
52	Return to Antioch via Caesarea and Jerusalem (Acts 18:18–22)
52/53–57	Third Missionary Period
53–56	Ministry in Ephesus (Acts 18:23—19:41)
56–57	Administering the Collection
57	Journey to Jerusalem and Arrest (Acts 20:3—21:36)
57–59	Caesarean Imprisonment and Paul's defense speeches (Acts 21:37—26:32)
59–60	Voyage to Rome (Acts 27:1—28:16)
60	Arrival in Rome (Acts 28:16)
60–62	House Arrest in Rome (Acts 28:17–31)

*Based on John Polhill, *Acts*, New American Commentary 26 (Nashville: Broadman Press, 1992).

Roman Emperors

A glimpse at the Roman emperors will give you a broader context for understanding the New Testament events.

1. Augustus Caesar (27 B.C.E. to 14 C.E.)
2. Tiberius Caesar (14–37 C.E.)
3. Gaius (Caligula) (37–41 C.E.)
4. Claudius (41–54 C.E.)
5. Nero (54–68 C.E.)
6. Vespasian (69–79)
7. Titus (79–81)
8. Domitian (81–96)
9. Nerva (96–98)
10. Trajan (98–117)
11. Hadrian (117–138)

Roman Government

Organization to protect *Pax Romana,* the Peace of Rome

1. Senatorial provinces under Proconsuls (see Acts 18:12)
2. Imperial provinces under emperor and procurators (Matthew 27:11)

Reflection Arising from Historical Study

1. Historical study thrusts the Bible student into the midst of the life situations of the writer and of the times the writer describes. Continual

historical study leads the reader to understand biblical passages from the author and participants' perspective rather than from a modern or postmodern perspective.

2. Historical study leads the Bible student to understand the types of historical sources available to the biblical writers. Oral literature, even literature used for entertainment, can be incorporated into the written documents that comprise our Bible so as to record the history of the people of God.

3. Historical study shows that the biblical writer may live even centuries after the history being narrated. Using proper oral and written sources in an oral literature culture under divine leadership can produce historical writing long after the fact.

4. Historical study finds that historical writing is never neutral. Historians write to interpret history and to use past history for contemporary purposes. Historians write out of a context and into a context in an effort to change or reinforce attitudes and actions in the context addressed.

5. Historical study shows that even documents in the "historical books" may have been penned for major reasons other than simply to record history. Writing is done to change opinions, to support one religious, social, or political group against another, to teach theological truth, or to warn of the dangers of following certain courses of action.

6. Historical study finds historical information in types of literature other than history writing. Prophecy, cultic poetry, letters, and other types of literature may provide facts and responses to a situation that are valuable for a historian even though the writer had a totally different purpose.

7. Historical study seeks to reconstruct a historical narrative that comes as close as possible to describing the past situation, viewpoints, and actions. Such study also seeks to disclose the historians' purpose(s) for writing. The purpose tells current readers as much about the historical situation as does a collection of "historical facts."

CHAPTER 5: Theological

Devotional

Textual

Literary

Exegetical

Historical

Finding the Bible's Teaching and Meaning

Theological Study

Ultimately, all types of Bible study lead to a Christian world view. This view comprises the lessons one learns about the nature of God, people, the universe, sin, salvation, ethics, etc. Strictly, theology is the study of God. More generally, it refers to all study directed at forming a world view dominated by a vision and understanding of God. Contemporary Bible students read the entire Bible to gather as much insight as possible into the various truths and principles that the Bible teaches. Ideally, the student would read each passage of Scripture, note the major teaching and secondary teaching of that passage, and then collect together all the passages that relate to each subdivision of theology. Examining what each passage says on the subject can lead to an overview of the biblical teaching on that particular subject. Until one has developed a personal theology from biblical study, one has not completed Bible study. That is a major reason Bible study is an ongoing, never-ending calling.

No one passage provides all the teaching the Bible seeks to impart on any one subject. Indeed, each passage adds its important nuance to the total biblical teaching. The student of the Bible faces the enormous task of finding other passages in the Bible that deal with the same theme, then fitting them together into a coherent whole that lets us see a theological teaching in its complexity rather than in some simplicity we might impose upon it.

As with other types of Bible study, theological study involves answering central questions of the Bible.

1. What categories will I use as I search the Scripture for meaning and a world view?

2. How does the biblical writer do theology?

3. What major theological truths or principles come from this passage? Are the truths you discover actually the intent of the writer or simply an exposition of your traditional theology?

4. Does the teaching in this passage agree with your theology, help change your theology, or sidetrack you a moment to prepare you for later teaching that will clarify what seems to be said here?

5. How does the theological teaching bring you into closer relationship with God? How does the teaching help you avoid temptation? How does the teaching show you ways to obey God that you have not previously attempted? How does the teaching help you praise and worship God? How does the teaching help you affirm yourself as a person made in God's image and being conformed into Christ's image?

Again we will look at Joshua 2, Psalm 137, Mark 8, and Philippians 2 to find answers. This time we will leave Mark 8 for your personal study. First, we will provide a preliminary answer to question one and show where to begin to gather the most significant Old Testament theological passages.

As a starting point, you may look for the following categories of teaching:

A. The Trinitarian God

B. The World and its Inhabitants

C. The Knowledge of God

D. God's Saving Purpose: Justification, Sanctification, Glorification

E. God's People: The Church

F. The Church and the World

G. Eschatology: The World's Final Experiences

You can then subdivide the major categories:

A. The Trinitarian God: Exodus 32:14; Deuteronomy 6:4; 29:20; Psalms 42; 86:10; Isaiah 45—46; 51; Matthew 28:19–20; John 10:30; 17:21–23; Acts 17:16–34; 1 John 4:7–21

1. God the Father: Exodus 34:4–16; 2 Corinthians 5:16–21

2. God the Son

3. God the Holy Spirit

B. The World and Its Inhabitants: Genesis 1—2; Psalm 19; Isaiah 45; Romans 1; 8:18–25

1. Creation

2. Natural Law and Miracles

3. Humanity

4. Sin: Genesis 3; 10; Romans 3:23; 6:23

5. Evil and Suffering: Job

C. The Knowledge of God: Exodus 24:4; 2 Samuel 22; Psalm 18; 139; Proverbs 1:1; 25:1; Jeremiah 36; Matthew 26:36–46; John 17:17; Acts 9; Romans 1; Galatians 2; 1 Timothy 3:14—4:5; Hebrews 11; 1 Peter 1:25

1. The Bible: The Revealed Word

2. Revelation: God's Initiative

3. History: The Context and Means of Revelation

D. God's Saving Purpose: Justification, Sanctification, Glorification: Exodus 15; Isaiah 45; Psalm 62; Luke 1; Acts 4:12; Romans 1:16; 10:10

1. Election

2. Provision

3. Human Response

4. Sanctification

5. Glorification

6. Discipleship

7. Ethics

8. Stewardship

E. God's People: The Church

   1. Old Testament People of God

   2. Purpose and Functions of the Church

   3. Ordinances in the Church

   4. Worship in the Church

   5. Proclamation in the Church

   6. Prayer by the Church

   7. Leaders of the Church

   8. Education for the Church

   9. The Family and the Church

F. The Church and the World

   1. Evangelism by the Church

   2. Missions throughout the World

G. Eschatology: The World's Final Experiences: Matthew 24—25; Mark 13; John 14; 2 Thessalonians; Revelation

   1. Death and Resurrection

   2. The Return of Christ

   3. The Final Resurrection

   4. Final Judgment

   5. The Eternal State: Saved, Lost, the Created World

   6. Eschatology's Call to Holiness

As you study Scripture, you will want to fill in the various theological categories with appropriate Scripture references. Another way to start is to read the Bible through, perhaps in a yearly program, and mark the major theological statements you see. Then you can go through and place them in the guide.

As a starting point, we will provide you one possible list of major Old Testament theological passages:

Basic Theological Passages of Scripture

1. Genesis 1—12; 15; 17; 26:1–5; 28:10–15; 48:8—49:27; 50:13–26

2. Exodus 3—4; 6; 12; 14—15; 18—20; 24; 32—34; 40:34–38

3. Leviticus 16; 18:1–5; 19:1–4

4. Numbers 6:22–27; 7:89; 11—14; 16:1–40; 22—24; 27

5. Deuteronomy 4—6; 10:12–22; 11; 17:14–20; 18:15–22; 29—30; 34

6. Joshua 1; 4—5; 8:30–35; 10:40; 11:15–23; 21:43–45; 23—24

7. Judges 2:1—3:11; 6:36–40; 8:22–28; 9:7–21; 21:25

8. Ruth 1; 4

9. 1 Samuel 3; 8; 12; 13:13–14; 15; 16; 18:1–4; 20

10. 2 Samuel 1—2; 7; 12; 15:1–12; 22; 23:1–7

11. 1 Kings 1:1—2:12; 3:10–15; 8:1–61; 9:1–9; 11:1—13, 29–40; 12:1–24; 13; 14:1–18; 18—19; 21

12. 2 Kings 2; 5; 10:18–28; 12:4–18; 17; 18—20; 21:1–15; 22—23; 24:20; 25:27–30

13. 1 Chronicles 11:1–9; 14:8–17; 16:7–36; 17; 21:1 (see 2 Sam. 24:1); 21:7–17; 22; 28; 29:10–20

14. 2 Chronicles 1:1—2:6; 5:11–14; 6:1—7:3; 7:11–22; 9:5–8; 10:15–16; 12:1–8; 13:1–18; 15; 16:7–9; 18; 19:5–11; 20:5–19; 21:7; 23:16–17; 24:17–22; 25:5–10, 14–16; 28:9–15; 29:5–19; 30:5–9, 12, 17–22; 31:10; 32:7–8, 25; 33:1–13; 34:22–28; 35:18–24; 36:12–23

15. Ezra 1:2–4; 3:10–13; 5:1–5; 6:6–12; 7:23–28; 9:4—10:5; 10:11–12

16. Nehemiah 1:4–11; 2:8, 18–20; 4:4–6, 14–15, 20; 5:8–13, 19; 6:9–14; 8:5–12, 17–18; 9:1–38; 10:28–39; 13:14, 22, 25–30

17. Esther 1:17–20; 2:10, 20; 3:2, 6, 8–10; 4:1, 13–14; 6:6–14; 7:4; 8:1–7; 9:20–26

18. Job 1:1—3:26; 7:21; 9:2–3; 9:25–35; 10:8–22; 13:7–28; 14:7–17; 16:13–22; 19:23–29; 23:1–7; 28—29; 31; 38—42

19. Psalms 1; 2; 8; 9:7–12; 14; 15; 16:5–11; 18; 19; 22; 23; 24; 25; 32; 33; 34; 45; 46; 47; 49; 50; 51; 58:1–5; 67; 69; 72:18–19; 75:12–17; 78:5–8, 37–39, 65–72; 82; 84; 85; 86; 89; 90; 95; 96; 99; 100; 103; 104; 105; 106; 107; 110; 115; 116; 119:9–16, 97–104; 121; 130; 135; 136; 137; 139; 145; 146; 150

20. Proverbs 1; 2; 3; 6; 8; 10; 14; 31

21. Ecclesiastes 1; 3; 5; 12

22. Song of Solomon (Song of Songs) 7

23. Isaiah 1; 2; 5; 6; 7:10–16; 9:1–7; 11:1–9; 22:15–23; 26:11–21; 28:1–8, 14–22; 29:13–14; 30:15–18; 32; 33:15–24; 40; 41:8–20; 42:1–9; 43:1–7, 10–13; 44:1–8, 21–28; 45:1–13, 20–25; 46; 49:1–7, 14–17; 51:9–11; 52:1–12; 52:13—53:12; 55; 56:1–8; 57:14–21; 58; 59; 60; 61; 63:7–14; 65:17–25; 66:1–2, 18–24

24. Jeremiah 1; 2:9–13, 26–28; 5:7–9; 6:9–15; 7; 8:18–22; 9:23–26; 10:6–16; 11:18—12:6; 13:20–25; 14:13–18; 15:1–4; 15:10–21; 16:1–4, 14–15; 17:5–10, 12–18; 18:1–12, 18–23; 20:7–18; 21:8–12; 22:1–9, 13–17; 23:3–8, 16–40; 24:5–7; 25:8–13; 26:1–6, 7–24; 27:16–18; 28; 29:4–7; 30:9–11; 31:1–6, 15–20, 27–37; 32:6–15, 27, 36–44; 33:3, 14–26; 36:20–32; 38:17–18; 39:11–12; 42:1–17; 43:10; 44:12–23; 50:27, 34; 51:15–20

25. Lamentations 2:1–4, 17; 3:8, 18, 19–44; 5:19–21

26. Ezekiel 1; 2—3; 5; 8; 9; 10; 11:16–21; 12:24–28; 13; 14:14–20; 16; 17:18–20; 18; 20; 22:23–31; 24:15–24; 28:1–10; 33:1–20; 34; 36:22–28; 37:1–14; 37:24–28; 38:23; 39:7, 22–29

27. Daniel 2:17–23, 27–30, 37–38, 44, 47; 3:16–18, 25–30; 4:1–3, 25–27, 34–37; 5:11–12, 17–18, 22–23; 6:10, 16, 22–23, 26–27; 7:13–14, 18, 27; 9:3–19

28. Hosea 1; 2:14–23; 4:1–3, 6–10, 15; 5:6; 6:4–11; 7:11–16; 8:1–7; 10:12–13; 11:1–11; 12:6; 13:14; 14:1–8

29. Joel 1:13–15; 2:1–2, 11, 12–17, 26–32; 3:10, 14–17

30. Amos 2:4–16; 3:2, 7–8; 4:1–13; 5:4–15, 18–24; 6:1–7; 7:1–9, 10–17; 8:4–6, 11–14; 9:4–13

31. Obadiah 15

32. Jonah 1:14, 16; 2:6–9; 3:8–10; 4:2–3, 10–11

33. Micah 2:1–3, 6–7, 11; 3:1–12; 4:1–8, 12; 5:2–3; 6:1–8; 7:7, 9–10, 18–20

34. Nahum 1:1–8

35. Habakkuk 1:1–6, 11–14; 2:4, 14, 20; 3:1–19

36. Zephaniah 1:7, 12, 14–15, 18; 2:3; 3:5, 9–13, 17

37. Haggai 1:3–8, 12–13; 2:4–9

38. Zechariah 1:1–6; 2:5, 7–13; 3:2; 4:6; 6:11–15; 7:9–10; 8:7–8, 14–17, 20–23; 9:9–10; 10:6, 12; 12:1, 10; 13:9; 14:6–9

39. Malachi 1:2–3, 14; 2:4–8, 10, 16; 3:1, 5–6, 7–10, 18; 4:2, 5–6

You will want to follow certain simple guidelines as you study a passage theologically:
Here are some ABCs of theological digging:

a. What does this particular verse exactly *say about God*?

b. What does this particular verse *imply about God and our relationship to him*?

c. Does this verse in itself give you enough information to *form a conclusion about God*? If not, *look further* and deeper in the Bible.

Example: Joshua 2

Our previous work has shown us that Joshua 2 is a chapter that rests on oral tradition. Its repeated central theme is God's gift of the land to Israel. A secondary purpose is to encourage Israel to accept foreigners who have the courage to confess Yahweh as the one and only God. With this information and the other work we have done on Joshua 2, we will look at the theological key questions:

1. What categories will I use as I search the Scripture for meaning and a world view?

Joshua 2 requires us to look at the nature of God, history, and revelation. We may also want to consider the category of missions.

2. How does the biblical writer do theology?

The writer of Joshua 2 does theology in a unique fashion. He places his basic theological statement in the mouth of a foreign prostitute. He repeats the statement twice more to be sure the reader sees the major emphasis of the story. The very theological subject— God as giver and land as object of gift—leads the reader to reflect back on the land promise to Abraham and the other patriarchs and to make inferences about divine providence, human stewardship, divine grace, and election. Such inference must be done in light of other Scriptures that teach these theological truths more clearly and deeply.

3. What major theological truths or principles come from this passage? Are the truths you discover actually the intent of the writer or simply an exposition of your traditional theology?

The writer of Joshua 2 hides nothing of the intended theological message. This is not a parable or a riddle or a historical report from which the reader is supposed to draw an unspoken message. Rather, the writer states three times that Yahweh has given the land to Israel. Placing the major theological statement in the mouth of the foreign prostitute communicates clearly a new approach to foreigners. This group of aliens does not face the holy war ban of death. This group can be incorporated into Israel. Now Israel must consider what qualifications foreigners must meet to be included.

Such theological teaching is not what a reader would bring to the text. It represents a surprise that causes the reader to rethink one's attitude to foreigners and trust in God.

4. Does the teaching in this passage agree with your theology, help change your theology, or sidetrack you a moment to prepare you for later teaching that will clarify what seems to be said here?

The teaching agrees with what I state as my theology most of the time, but I must rethink my practice and see if this theology is put into action with people unlike me and my family. Here is a clear mission emphasis and a clear statement about the nature of God that the rest of Scripture will support over and over.

5. How does the theological teaching bring you into closer relationship with God? How does the teaching help you avoid temptation? How does the teaching show you ways to obey God in ways you have not previously done so? How does the teaching help you praise and worship God? How does the teaching help you affirm yourself as a person made in God's image and being conformed into Christ's image?

The teaching of God as giver and thus as owner of the land reaffirms the loving, giving nature of the God I know and reminds me of my duty to accept the divine gifts with humility and gratitude and to use them in God's service. Teaching on foreigners forces me to constantly review the prejudice I am tempted to feel and act on against people a bit unlike me. The teaching encourages me to reach out to people I am not familiar with and to join them in serving God by showing loving kindness and faithfulness to them in all relationships. Such an all-caring and all-providing God deserves praise and worship, not just routine and ritual. For God to give so much for me leads me to find what I can do and give for God and thus answer the divine mandate to take care of the earth God created for us.

Example: Psalm 37

Psalm 37 is a lament written by exiles in Babylon pledging loyalty to Jerusalem, worshiping Yahweh together in their anger and grief, and pleading to God for revenge on the cruel enemies.

1. What categories will I use as I search the Scripture for meaning and a world view?

The categories here come from the action and emotion of the passage rather than from objective statements. The psalmist participates in a worship service of lament and expresses his prayer of grief and anger to God. The categories become honesty and emotion in prayer and ways to deal with human anger and frustration. A secondary category is that of human dealings with enemies.

2. How does the biblical writer do theology?

The writer does theology in a secondary mode by lifting curses, oaths, and angry desires to God. By so doing, the psalmist demonstrates how to handle human emotion in relationship to God through prayer and trust. The content of the prayer if actually carried out would be terrible theology, but in the context of lamentation and prayer, it becomes another way to show trust in God and to deal with the dark feelings of the heart.

3. What major theological truths or principles come from this passage? Are the truths you discover actually the intent of the writer or simply an exposition of your traditional theology?

The psalmist teaches the nature of sincere prayer. The poet does not blatantly attempt to teach theology so much as to carry out a relationship with God that becomes an example for everyone who reads the psalm as the readers deal with similar emotions and desperate situations.

4. Does the teaching in this passage agree with your theology, help change your theology, or sidetrack you a moment to prepare you for later teaching that will clarify what seems to be said here?

The teaching in this psalm has given depth to my own prayer life and my theology of prayer. Remembering this psalm forces me to open my heart to God and call out the dark thoughts and feelings as well as the more generally pious thoughts I learn to pray from normal worship services. The psalm also leads me to attend to others in their anger and depression without trying to judge or change them.

5. How does the theological teaching bring you into closer relationship with God? How does the teaching help you avoid temptation? How does the teaching show you ways to obey God that you have not previously attempted? How does the teaching help you praise and worship God? How does the teaching help you affirm yourself as a person made in God's image and being conformed into Christ's image?

The psalm calls me to be angry and sin not. It frees me to share with God rather than to follow the crowd in trying to hide my darkest feelings and doubts from God. By shouting out with the psalmist those problems that vex and anger me, I find myself drawn much nearer to God because I trust God more. Eventually, the lament will lead to insight into God's actions on my behalf. At that point lament will turn to a deeper, more honest participation in worship and praise. When God listens to my anger over my wife's death or my loss of a job or a car wreck or my spat with a fellow employee, God shows me how much I am valued and so should value myself.

Example: Philippians 2

Philippians 2 has as its center a hymn to Christ calling us to imitate the life Christ lived in humbling himself and his status by coming down from the throne room of heaven to dwell as a human being among us humans. Its central purpose is to give us an example of humble living that we should follow. A strong secondary purpose is to describe the nature of Jesus the Messiah.

1. What categories will I use as I search the Scripture for meaning and a world view?

This small part of Paul's joyful letter to the Philippians joins heaven and earth as it proclaims the humble example of Jesus in coming to earth to bring us salvation and as it calls us to be true to that salvation. The categories thus become the mission and nature of Jesus and the definition of discipleship and ethics.

2. How does the biblical writer do theology?

Paul does theology in Philippians by writing a standard style letter to a church he loves and appreciates (not the case with all the churches to which he wrote, for Galatians and Corinthians are quite different). Having written an extensive thanksgiving and having described his own situation, he turns to practical teaching built on theology. He knows the church through practical experience and through reports from Epaphroditus. In prison and unable to visit the church, Paul teaches them through letters.

3. What major theological truths or principles come from this passage? Are the truths you discover actually the intent of the writer or simply an exposition of your traditional theology?

The most important teaching of the passage centers on the nature of Jesus Christ as equal with God but humble enough to become human. The precise teaching of the passage is the call for Christians to imitate Christ. The opening verses of the chapter show the nature of church and of the life of the believer joined in love and fellowship with the Godhead. These are explicitly stated by Paul.

4. Does the teaching in this passage agree with your theology, help change your theology, or sidetrack you a moment to prepare you for later teaching that will clarify what seems to be said here?

The depth of this teaching and its demand for giving attention to others rather than self is part of my intellectual theological belief, but day by day proves the difficulty of making theology come to life in relationships with God and with other people. Other passages of Scripture will certainly reinforce this teaching, but this is one of the more explicit passages concerning the dual nature of Jesus and the call to Christian humility.

5. How does the theological teaching bring you into closer relationship with God? How does the teaching help you avoid temptation? How does the teaching show you ways to obey God that you have not previously attempted? How does the teaching help you praise and worship God? How does the teaching help you affirm yourself as a person made in God's image and being conformed into Christ's image?

Meditation on the dual nature and self-emptying of Jesus brings new amazement and gratitude for who Jesus is and for what Jesus has done for me. Such insights into the nature of the second person of the Trinity always bring me closer to my Lord and yet always challenge me to avoid selfishness and the temptation to manipulate others. I tend to live a sheltered life with my books and computer, but I am called to get involved in the world where God is at work and show a life imitating Jesus to those who do not know him. When I answer Paul's letter with joy and follow his call to imitate Jesus, I become much more like Jesus and thus realize more and more that Christ is reforming me in his own image.

Exercise: Mark 8

What have you learned from Mark 8 in previous study? How do you answer these questions about Mark 8?

1. What categories will I use as I search the Scripture for meaning and a world view?

2. How does the biblical writer do theology?

3. What major theological truths or principles come from this passage? Are the truths you discover actually the intent of the writer or simply an exposition of your traditional theology?

4. Does the teaching in this passage agree with your theology, help change your theology, or sidetrack you a moment to prepare you for later teaching that will clarify what seems to be said here?

5. How does the theological teaching bring you into closer relationship with God? How does the teaching help you avoid temptation? How does the teaching show you ways to obey God that you have not previously attempted? How does the teaching help you praise and worship God? How does the teaching help you affirm yourself as a person made in God's image and being conformed into Christ's image?

Reflection Arising from Theological Study

1. After we learn something theological about God, we are faced with the *"triple A's"*:

   a. *Acknowledgment* of the Bible information as truth,
   b. *Acceptance* of the truth as our belief,
   c. *Action* on the belief as part of our lives.

2. Bible writers teach theology in many different ways—some through words, some through emotions, some through stories without an explicit moral statement, some through letters, some through literary structures. The list may be extended to great lengths. Having read and studied a passage, the Bible student must look back and determine how the writer is conveying his major theological teachings and principles.

3. Explicit major teachings in a passage often hook onto previous teachings or point forward to future fulfillment and understanding. Having discovered the major teaching of a passage, the student will want to discover links to previous and following passages. This is especially true in relationship to creation, exodus, conquest, messiah, deliverance, and salvation.

4. Major theological teachings often lead to theological implications that the reader must infer from the passage: *If God has done this, then God must be like this. If temptation comes in this way, then it must say something about human will, human nature, and sin.*

5. Theological discovery should lead to action in worship and in discipleship and ethics.

6. Theological study should do much more than reaffirm what someone else has taught you or what you have picked up in church tradition or popular reading. Theological study of the Bible should show you truth you have not known previously and draw you into a type of relationship with God that you have not enjoyed previously.

7. Theological study of Scripture is an ongoing challenge to learn more about God and the divine presence in the world and to conform to the theology you learn.

Going Deeper

Theological study may include word studies throughout Scripture if they are done carefully. The Bible student must pick a significant theological term, use an exhaustive concordance to determine which words are used in the original language, and then study each of the passages for the original language words separately.

I. I have studied most of the major passages that speak of the "word of God," the "word of the Lord," etc. A full listing would also look at the Law, the commandments, the judgments, promise, instruction, etc. See Psalm 119 for the most extensive praise of the word of God. Here are characteristics of the word of God:

A. Notice the call most often is to hear and obey the word of God. The Bible has much more to say about obeying the word of God than it does about defining and defending the nature of the word of God.

B. The word of God is both creative and destructive.

C. The word of God does not fail in its mission, but people can fail to carry out the mission given by the word of God.

D. The word of God is our offensive weapon in preaching and proclamation.

E. Humans can dishonor the word of God.

F. The word of God preached effectively brings growth.

G. The word of God endures forever.

H. The work of the word of God brings rejoicing and praise for the word of God from God's people.

I. We cannot take for granted that the word of God will always be available. God may hide it from a people who ignore or reject it.

J. The word teaches us the ways of God and leads us in God's paths.

K. The word retains appeal for the nations.

L. The word of God effectively proves itself to be God's word of truth.

M. Obeying the word of God brings reproach and derision from unbelievers and may lead to death.

N. Whatever its effect, the word of God is always good and upright or trustworthy.

O. The word of God always comes to fulfillment.

P. God's people should hold God's word in fearful awe and respect.

Q. God's word is a word of revelation.

R. The word of God is the divine guarantee of eternal life.

S. To keep God's word you must love Jesus.

T. The word of God is powerful.

U. Believing God's word leads to baptism.

V. The word of God is a healing word.

W. The word of God is a source of hope.

X. The word of God judges people's thoughts and intentions.

Y. The word of God brings the new birth.

Z. The word of God abides in believers.

AA. We can proclaim the word of God without fear.

II. The word of God was proclaimed and taught orally before much of it became written. The words of God proved themselves true, powerful, and authoritative in the life of the synagogue and the church before they became finally collected as the word of God in the form we know.

III. Theologians have used various passages of Scripture to create a theological vocabulary describing the word of God. Much of the vocabulary comes from the definition of God rather than from clear biblical statements about the Bible. Some of the most important terms, as defined by David Dockery, *Christian Scripture* (Nashville: B&H, 1995), include:

A. *Canon*: Refers to the group of books acknowledged by the early church as the rule of faith and practice.

    1. The Jewish canon has thirty-nine books when listed in the Christian form, but the *Jewish* canonical order is: five books of law, Joshua, Judges, Samuel, Kings, Isaiah, Jeremiah, Ezekiel, twelve "minor" prophets considered as one book; Psalms, Job, Proverbs, Ruth, Song of Songs, Ecclesiastes, Lamentations, Esther, Daniel, Ezra, Nehemiah, Chronicles.

2. The Christian canon adds twenty-seven books.

3. The Catholics add the Apocrypha as part of the Christian canon: 1st Esdras; 2nd Esdras; Tobit; Additions to Esther; Wisdom of Solomon; Ecclesiasticus (Wisdom of Jesus ben Sirach); Baruch; Letter of Jeremiah; Prayer of Azariah and the Song of the Three added to Daniel; Daniel and Susanna; Daniel, Bel, and the Snake (Dragon); The Prayer of Manasseh; First Maccabees; and Second Maccabees.

B. *Concursive Inspiration*: Inspired Scriptures are at the same time divine and human words. Scripture has a dual authorship, being a product of God as well as of human authors.

C. *Contextual*: Some portions of Scripture have adapted certain life situations or temporal contexts to communicate their message.

D. *Docetic view of Scripture*: a heresy that maintains that the human authorship of Scripture is only apparent or imaginative.

E. *Inerrancy*: The theological claim that when all the facts are known, the Bible (in its original autographs or form) when properly interpreted in light of the culture and the means of communication that had developed by the time of its composition, is completely true in all that it affirms, to the degree of precision intended by the author's purpose, in all matters relating to God and God's creation.

F. *Infallibility*: The theological claim that the Bible is incapable of error and cannot deceive or mislead. Some contemporary scholars want to apply the term "infallible" only to the message of the Bible to avoid the affirmation that the Bible is also truthful in matters relating to history, geography, and related matters; but that is not the classical view.

G. *Inspiration*: It is the superintending influence the Holy Spirit exerted on the biblical writers so that the accent and interpretation of God's revelation have been recorded as God intended so that the Bible is actually the word of God.

H. *Normative*: It indicates that the Scripture's power is not limited by temporal or contextual matters. The message of Scripture has binding authority for the contemporary church.

I. *Personal revelation*: It views revelation primarily as a personal experience or encounter with God in Christ. It focuses attention on the dynamic and personal characteristics of God's manifestation of himself to men and women.

J. *Plenary*: It comes from a Latin term meaning full and means that the Bible is inspired in all of its parts.

K. *Progressive revelation*: It indicates that God's self-disclosure unfolds and develops over time, interpreting and amplifying the previous revelation but not contradicting it in any way.

L. *Propositional revelation*: God's self-manifestation understood as information about God, including the divine interpretation of revelatory events. A proper view of Christian truth distinguishes between the personal and the propositional aspects but does not separate them.

M. *Revelation*: An uncovering, a removal of the veil, a disclosure of what was previously unknown and thus God's manifestation of Himself to humankind in such a way that men and women can know and have fellowship with Him.

N. *Sensus Plenior*: A Latin term indicating that God intended a fuller meaning of a passage of Scripture although that fuller meaning was not clearly understood by the human author or the original hearers/readers.

O. *Special Revelation*: God's self-manifestation in a particular way to particular people at particular times and places (often contrasted or coupled with general revelation as seen in creation and available to all people at all times).

P. *Theopneustos*: A Greek term translated "divinely inspired" or God-breathed (2 Timothy 3:16), indicating that the Scriptures are the product of God's creative breath and thus divine.

Q. *Typological interpretation*: A type of biblical interpretation in which persons, events, or things in the Old Testament are interpreted as foreshadowings of persons, events, or things in the New Testament. Typological interpretation differs from an allegorical one in that the latter sees the hidden meaning of a text, whereas the former understands a revelatory connection between two historically distinct but spiritually significant persons or events.

CHAPTER 6: Devotional

Textual

Literary

Exegetical

Historical

Theological

Finding the Personal Meaning of the Text

Devotional Study

Devotional study is the type of Bible reading most Christians engage in. They take a devotional guide put out by a local church, a denominational home office, or a religious press and follow its suggested readings more or less faithfully day by day. Then they read the short devotional in the guide and perhaps follow prayer suggestions from the guide. In so doing, they learn much, draw closer to God, and create good habits. But too often such devotional reading is far removed from whatever Bible study is done. We suggest that devotional study be connected to Bible study done in a small Bible study group or in a Sunday school class. Devote private devotional time each day to reading the Scripture you will be studying with the group. As you begin, find which type of study looks to prove the most interesting and profitable for that particular passage. Spend the week doing that kind of study, while at a different part of the day doing your devotional work on the same passage. As you become familiar with the various types of study, you will want to add one or more types of study for the week's passage. But never eliminate your devotional study. Using the other methods of study will help you see the major theme of the passage and the major applications for your life. Occasionally, God may surprise you with an "aha" moment in which some word or verse says something in particular to you even if it is not connected to the main thrust of the passage. Never get so tied to a way of studying Scripture that you miss a special word God has for you.

As with other methods, devotional study is best done through asking and answering basic questions:

1. Which character in the passage do you identify with?

2. What do you discover as the central teaching of the passage? As the week progresses, do you see different nuances of this teaching or an entirely different teaching within the passage?

3. What warning does the narrative give you?

4. What promise or hope does the narrative stir in your life?

5. What response of obedience does the narrative call on you to make?

6. How does the passage deepen your personal relationship with God?

7. What words of the narrative catch your attention at this particular point in your life to give you a special message from God? How will you share God's message to you with the Bible study group?

Example: Joshua 2

1. Which character in the passage do you identify with?

The choices are clear: Joshua, spies, Rahab, king's messengers, first audience. It is difficult to identify with Joshua, the almost perfect leader of God's people. While on the mission field, I felt somewhat like Rahab, a person who confessed the same God but lived surrounded by people whose ancestors had served God long before I came along and in a way quite distinct from the way I served. I found it difficult to be accepted in that culture and body of believers. At times, I identify with the king's messengers, trying to fulfill an assignment and making a total mess out of it. Often, my mission appears to be that of the spies—carry out orders as commanded. All the while, I know I am supposed to join the audience to whom the passage is delivered and see if I can be as quietly obedient as the spies, as courageous as Rahab with her confession of faith, and as faithful as Joshua in listening to God and commanding the Israelite people. The person(s) I identify with today may be different by the end of the week or month as circumstances and situations change. Identifying with someone in the passage helps me get more deeply involved in what is happening and the emotions that are felt and expressed.

2. What do you discover as the central teaching of the passage? As the week progresses, do you see different nuances of this teaching or an entirely different teaching within the passage?

The central teaching at first reading calls forth the faithfulness and courage of Rahab as an example for us to follow. Closer reading begins to see the emphasis on God's giving of the land and drives me to meditate on the providence of God and the divine goodness in fulfilling promises and giving what we need when we need it. All the while in the back of my mind runs the theme of treatment of foreigners who respond to divine actions with faith and the fear of God. How open am I to people culturally distinct from me, my church, and my friends.

3. What warning does the narrative give you?

Joshua 2 warns me to listen and learn about God from people whom I often ignore and even put down. I have learned so much from so many throughout Europe, in Israel, in eastern Africa, in the former Czechoslovakia, in India, and farther around the earth. I have additionally learned by worshiping and socializing with tenant farmers, African Americans, Latinos, and many other groups. The academic study of Europeans, the loud joy of Kenyans at worship, the warmth and depth of emotion in African American worship, and the hunger for truth in the Latino and Asian churches—all these warn me not to take religion and worship so matter-of-factly and not to use my scholarly credentials to brush others off as somehow not my equals. Günter, Na'em, Samson, Pablo, the Gregories, and Brother Smith head the list of hundreds who have brought me down from my high horse to remember God can communicate with, and get through to, a prostitute when self-proclaimed people of God only go through the motions of confession, faith, and obedience.

4. What promise or hope does the narrative stir in your life?

The passage promises me that God will fulfill every promise that ever issued from our God to the people of God. I do not need to worry about God's faithfulness, only my own. Even when I am a stranger in a foreign land trying to accomplish what the land's residents do not really want, I can share the good news of God's promises and know that God will have people ready to trust those promises and help me share them.

5. What response of obedience does the narrative call on you to make?

The passage calls on me to trust God more fully, to obey completely as did Joshua and the spies, and to go where God sends even if that proves to be to a place or with a people that makes me feel uncomfortable or unequipped for service. Even as I advance in age, I must look for God's call to mission and answer it, even if it carries me across the oceans to people whose language I do not speak and whose culture I do not understand. I must let God take away my fears and step out in faith.

6. How does the passage deepen your personal relationship with God?

Joshua 2 hits me anew with the faithfulness of God and calls me to share Rahab's confession of faith. Only as I constantly repeat what I believe about God and what I know God is about to do to fulfill promises to me can I draw nearer to God and feel the safety of divine presence. When I trust that God is who Rahab proclaimed God to be, then I find my faith stronger and my relationship closer.

7. What words of the narrative catch your attention at this particular point in your life to give you a special message from God? How will you share God's message to you with the Bible study group?

"The house of a prostitute" catches my eye because it reminds me how quick I am to render judgment against other people because of certain ways they act, certain professions they are in, certain language they use, or certain failures and lies I have discovered in their relationships with me. I need to give up my judge's robes and let God handle all the details of judgment. I need to forgive and to use the opportunity to dig deeper into my own life to see where I need to ask forgiveness.

Example: Mark 8

1. Which character in the passage do you identify with?

The choices may be greater than meets the eye at first glance: Jesus, friends of the blind man, crowd that followed Jesus, disciples, Peter, and Mark's original audience. The biggest temptation is to sit back as an objective observer and identify with Jesus, your hero and Savior. Such a holy, aloof stance lets us admire Jesus and ignore the warnings of the passage. One could choose to identify with the friends who brought the blind man and see oneself as always willing to help others. Thus you exit the story feeling good about yourself and amazed at what Jesus can do. This may be the stance to take if you have never believed on Jesus. If so, you need to take the next step to trust Jesus and ask him to be your Lord and Savior. You may identify with the blind man as helpless, with no way to improve your lot. Jesus offers hope for such helpless people. You can call on him now to heal your troubled soul. You may identify with Peter, struggling to understand who Jesus is and expecting much more than a road of suffering leading crossward. As Peter, you may make the right confession of faith but not fully understand what you are saying. You may find something about the Jesus narrative that just does not fit who you are and who you expect Jesus to be. Mark would point you to the disciple band as a whole. As one of the disciples, you are much like

Peter in your feelings. You just do not have the personality to express it so quickly and abruptly. You signed on with Jesus to find peace and blessing. Now he tells you to find suffering and even death on the road crossward. You must decide whether to return home and forget the quest or to follow Jesus to Jerusalem, a bit fearful of where Jesus is leading you. Is your discipleship comparable to the blind man after Jesus' first application: see better but not well enough to be satisfied? Continue reading your Bible and ask a Bible study friend to help you understand who Jesus is and why you should follow him.

2. What do you discover as the central teaching of the passage? As the week progresses, do you see different nuances of this teaching or an entirely different teaching within the passage?

First reading points to Jesus' ability to heal and the disciples' confession of Jesus as Messiah. First reading also calls one to take up the cross to follow Jesus. This also brings a bit of confusion. How do these stories all fit together? Why does Jesus require two tries to heal for the only time in the gospels? How do the questions about the miraculous feedings fit into all this? We must read again and look deeper to find the structure that blends the stories together. Devotional reading becomes more than a quick glance at a couple of verses. Devotional reading becomes a search for structure and wholeness that lets us hear and respond to the passage's deeper message. The miracle story becomes not just another instance of Jesus showing his power to the people. Jesus' miracle becomes a symbol uniting the first half of Mark's gospel with the journey to the cross. The story tests our spiritual eyesight. How clearly do we see Jesus? What part of Jesus' demands do we want to remain blind to? Do we think we have traveled further down the Jesus road as believers than we really have? What is lacking in our understanding of Jesus and in our discipleship?

3. What warning does the narrative give you?

Second and third reading and meditation on structure bring warning loud and clear. I must not see myself as too secure and too advanced in my discipleship. Jesus demands more than following him to an eternal throne. He calls on me to be ready to die for him. This warning accepts no easy, flippant response. I must dig into my soul to discover how truly committed I am to Jesus.

4. What promise or hope does the narrative stir in your life?

This passage does not offer easy, immediate hope. Mark 8 places a large cross at the end of the road to hope. I must test myself and let Jesus test me. Jesus is coming in glory with his angels. I want to be part of that coming, but first I must have faith that is willing to die the most horrible of deaths, not selfish ambition that wants to sit at Christ's right hand as he establishes an earthly kingdom.

5. What response of obedience does the narrative call on you to make?

I must pledge to follow Jesus through sickness and health, through popularity and rejection, through prosperity and poverty, through power and weakness, through safe times and dangerous ones, through life to the cross of a martyr's death. I must do more than say, "Jesus is the Messiah." I must follow the footsteps of Jesus, which lead not to Jerusalem's throne but to Calvary's hill.

6. How does the passage deepen your personal relationship with God?

This passage leads me either to cement my relationship with God so that it becomes stronger than ever before, or it leads me to back off the religious stuff and follow at a distance, waiting to see what will truly happen before I commit myself. Only as I walk through the pain of the cross may I hope to participate in the glory of resurrection and the power of Pentecost.

7. What words of the narrative catch your attention at this particular point in your life to give you a special message from God? How will you share God's message to you with the Bible study group?

"Peter began to rebuke him." I can never get these words out of my mind. How audacious could Peter be? How assured was he that he knew the Messiah's road so well that he could warn Jesus not to take a detour. Am I too quick to show the meaning of a passage to others that I forget its true meaning for me? Do I really, deep down, follow Jesus only for the glory of earthly power and prestige, so that, when he leads me through the valley of the shadow of death, I will truly be afraid and try to turn back in another direction? Is my theology so set that I cannot learn, even from Jesus?

Example: Philippians 2

1. Which character in the passage do you identify with?

The choice is quite limited. I can identify with Paul, with Epaphroditus, or with the Philippian church. To identify with Paul is simplest at first glance. I am a mature Christian leader and want to rejoice with my church and show them how great Christ is. But to do so, I must endure persecution and imprisonment. Identity with Epaphroditus forces me out of the spotlight to play the messenger's role between Paul and the church. This calls on me to embark on dangerous travels, join Paul in prison, endure sickness, and faithfully carry Paul's message back to the church. Am I willing to do this for only the briefest of recognition and gratitude? Or must I force myself more clearly to the spotlight so people will fawn over me in special ways? To identify with the church is to be a willing steward, sharing my possessions with the needy, to be honestly concerned and involved with people undergoing suffering and persecution, to be loyal to a caring pastor even when he has departed the scene, to express great joy and gladness over the gospel and what it means to me, and to be willing to listen when God has given someone a message for our church. Interestingly, Paul calls on the Philippians to identify with Jesus—not in his glorious divinity, but in his humble humanity, giving up power and glory and comfort to walk Galilee's dusty roads and eventually turn to the cross and die that we might have eternal life. Am I willing to identify with Christ in emptying myself of power and position to serve God and do the divine will, whatever it might be?

2. What do you discover as the central teaching of the passage? As the week progresses, do you see different nuances of this teaching or an entirely different teaching within the passage?

The passage tells me about the marvelous sacrifice of Jesus. He emptied himself. He humbled himself. He obeyed God even to the point of allowing himself to be crucified on the cross. Still, God in divine greatness exalted Jesus, raising him back to heaven, where eventually everyone will recognize how great Jesus is and will fall down in worship.

A second reading stops me quick. Before I get to the marvelous hymn about Christ, I find Paul's call to me to work for unity in the church even when it means letting someone else carry the day with his or her ideas and programs. Christ's example should lead me to do this humble act? Jesus himself! If Jesus is Lord, then I must be a slave. That puts the passage in a whole new light. If I want love, mercy, fellowship, encouragement, affection, then I must put others' interests ahead of my own agenda.

3. What warning does the narrative give you?

The warning glares at me: give up your pride and selfishness. Live for the good of others, not for yourself. Be like Christ, not like the world.

4. What promise or hope does the narrative stir in your life?

Christ is exalted on high. He waits for me to join him after I have finished my life as a slave to Christ and his church.

5. What response of obedience does the narrative call on you to make?

I must hand over everything I am and have to Christ and the church. I must be a source of encouragement, love, and affection to fellow believers. I must become a slave and empty myself of all ownership and power. I must do God's plan, not mine.

6. How does the passage deepen your personal relationship with God?

The magnificence of Christ's sacrifice becomes clearer and clearer every time I read this passage. I fall down before the Messiah and praise and thank him for becoming a slave to die for my sins. I again commit all I have to Christ and seek to follow his example.

7. What words of the narrative catch your attention at this particular point in your life to give you a special message from God? How will you share God's message to you with the Bible study group?

"Emptied himself" always catches my eye. It quickly carries me back to seminary days and the exalted talk about "kenosis" christology. Then I settle back to earth and see that emptying by Jesus serves as my call to be a slave. I so greedily soak up honors, positions, praise, and accomplishment. I need so to go to the backroads of town and find the least of these my brothers and do unto them as I would want them to do to me.

Now it is your time to study a passage devotionally. How do you answer the questions applied to this passage?

Exercise: Psalm 137

1. Which character in the passage do you identify with?

2. What do you discover as the central teaching of the passage? As the week progresses, do you see different nuances of this teaching or an entirely different teaching within the passage?

3. What warning does the narrative give you?

4. What promise or hope does the narrative stir in your life?

5. What response of obedience does the narrative call on you to make?

6. How does the passage deepen your personal relationship with God?

7. What words of the narrative catch your attention at this particular point in your life to give you a special message from God? How will you share God's message to you with the Bible study group?

Reflection Arising from Devotional Study

1. Devotional study should lead me to find a character involved in the narrative or other type of literature that I can identify with. Reading the same passage at different times may lead me to identity with different characters. I must see how their relationships to God and their reactions to God's acts and words compare to my situation and my responses.

2. Devotional study is more than simply reading a passage quickly and uttering a familiar prayer. Devotional study asks me to read carefully and find the key teaching(s) in the passage.

3. Devotional study may best be done in conjunction with Bible study done for study groups or Sunday school.

4. Devotional study looks for warnings, promises, and calls to obedience in the passage so that I may make an explicit response to the passage and then check myself to see if I am living out that hope, that promise, or that warning to obey.

5. Devotional study's central aim is to build relationship with God. Day by day you should find yourself becoming more observant of Bible truths, promises, and warnings. Day by day you should find yourself responding in obedience and being drawn closer to the God of the universe. Relationship with God does not come by fulfilling the duty of daily Bible reading. Relationship with God comes by listening to the message of Scripture and obeying what God reveals to you in that Scripture.

6. At times, God will surprise you with a special word that precisely fits your situation today. That surprise may be far removed from the original meaning of a scripture, but is suited by God just for you today. Do not be so stuck to a method of study that you miss divine delights as God surprises you with a true word for today.

Conclusion

We have carefully followed the Bible study road down various paths to learn the deeper meanings of the Word. Textual study has shown us how God preserved the biblical Word even when human copyists and teachers did not always copy it or transmit it exactly the same way. It offers us a chance to be detectives and search out clues that lead us as close as possible to the original writing of the text.

Literary studies help us get into the author's mind and skill set to see the kind of literature the author produced. Poetry, often marked by parallelism, uses figures of speech and symbolism to get at the emotional and meaning level of events. Hyperbole and analogy often mark such recitation of history. In standard prose, a much more straightforward report of events meets the reader. Still, the writing provides more than a list of objective events or minute-by-minute descriptions of action, reaction, and interaction. Narrative prose presents one perspective and one person's reflections and interpretation of an event, written down for specific purposes in relationship to the audience.

Prose writing comes in many literary forms utilized for many purposes. Prose writing may seek religious reform or political change. Prose writing may produce propaganda for or against internal or external groups or practices. Prose writing may reflect a cultic ritual or a personal perspective. Thus we follow basic questions to seek to determine the kind of literature involved, the purpose in writing the literature, and the possibility or intentionality of using that type of literature to report history. One does not use science fiction techniques to write modern or ancient history. A short story is usually thought to reflect a writer's imagination, but may well be based on historical experience. A novel or novella more often uses characterization and plot resolution to teach moral truths or to point in moral directions rather than to tediously insure that the narrative is the facts and nothing but the facts. Literary study thus opens up some expectations for the reader while eliminating other expectations. Literary study lets the Bible student appreciate the literary greatness of biblical writers without placing undue restraints on them.

Exegetical study seeks to find the meaning of the text by examining its larger context, its significant parts, and its current structure. Exegesis works on the basis of textual and literary study to determine what the words of the text can mean, how they can be variously translated, how the syntax can be differently interpreted, how the passage fits into the larger structure of the book, and how the structure of the passage itself shows the central meaning and purpose of the passage. Exegetical study helps the Bible student determine the important message of the passage and the structures and terms used to add emphasis outside the main theme. Joined with textual and literary results, exegetical study gives you a sure footing for explaining the original meaning of the text in relationship to its original audience. Meaning grows out of the relationship between the writer with his message and the audience with their needs.

Historical study sets the writer, the writer's sources, and the book in specific contexts. This helps one see the power of the passage's contents as it develops from oral recitation to written form to inclusion in a biblical book. Historical study depends on textual, literary, and exegetical studies to determine the text, the literary type, and the central meaning of a text to determine one's expectations as to the author's use of the material in historical narration. Certainly Jotham's fable of the ruling trees (Judges 9) does not arouse historical expectations that a briar bush was crowned king and reigned. It does point to a surviving son mocking his murderous brother as a strong historical possibility. Historical study shows the writer's skill in bringing together eyewitness reports, oral tradition, written reports, or whatever sources are available to portray significant and insignificant characters as heroes or villains and ultimately to demonstrate how God used such characters for divine purposes. Only as one looks at the literary and historical results can one determine that this report is expected to be straightforward history, though it is written in ironic style with tongue in cheek to portray characters and/or events ideally or utterly negatively, quite distorted from the character's own self-image or self-portrayal. Thus, in their *own* minds Abimelech and Samson in Judges work as heroes to restore justice for the little people of the land, while the biblical writers present them as selfish egotists working only for their own reputations to gain revenge on peoples who wronged them.

Theological study helps us put the entire Bible together according to its major teachings. This is a lifelong process of finding the central themes of biblical passages and uniting them with other passages dealing with the same themes. It involves exacting word study to ensure the Bible student is placing similar *themes* together rather than just placing similar *words* together even when the words have different meanings in different passages. A simple illustration of this would be to study "sleep" and "asleep" in 1 Thessalonians 4 and 5 as if the term always meant "physically dead" when some of the meanings here are "morally dead," "not open to God's direction in life," and "not acting as a believer should act." Such theological study will give us a framework for a world view and an ethical stance with which to face a world opposed to such ethics.

Finally, devotional study brings all Bible study to the personal heart, helping the student to personalize study and see how the Bible reading cements one's relationship with God, provides an area of life in which to improve one's faithfulness and thus show openness to God's Word, and perhaps surprises one with a special word into a personal crisis the devotional student faces today or this week. Devotional study lies on a foundation of the other five types of study so that the reader of the Bible truly begins to see what kind of message the Bible delivers on an ongoing basis rather than looking for a personal surprise every time the reader picks up the Scriptures. The ongoing biblical message helps build the strong, ongoing relationship with God on a stronger foundation than the hit-or-miss, surprise-finding devotional reading.

May these pointers to six ways to study the Bible become God's instrument in opening the meaning of Scripture to your life. May they help you reject opinions that misrepresent what Scripture says. May this type of study send you looking for new truth that will tie you closer to God rather than sending you on wild goose chases after questions and meanings whose answers the Bible never intended to reveal.

May God bless you as you read and study, and may your reading, study, and life bring glory and honor and praise to our God.

Going Deeper

Your turn now! How do you start your Bible study?

First, choose a passage for study, preferably one you are studying with a small Bible study group or Sunday school.

Next, read through the entire book the passage appears in to see:

1. The major themes
2. Structural markers
3. Featured theological issues
4. Basic outline of book
5. Verses central to theme and structure

Third, find an opening structural marker separating the passage from what precedes it.

Fourth, find a closing structural marker separating the passage from what follows.

Fifth, read as many translations as possible (four or five is good) to detect significant translation differences or textual problems.

Use a concordance to determine as far as possible why the differences exist; use footnotes to see if the translation has followed a different manuscript.

Next, outline the chronological line the passage presents—watch for flashbacks or predictions or other elements out of chronological sequence.

Finally, outline the development of the basic theme or issue in the passage—in narrative go from the statement of the problem to its resolution, if it is resolved here.

Bible Tools Worksheet

Complete the following worksheet

1. *Center Column Reference System*
    a. Is found… (*where?*)

    b. Provides the following information
        1)

        2)

        3)

2. *Small Concordance*
    a. Is found… (*where?*)

    b. Provides the following information
        1)

        2)

        3)

    c. More of the same type of information is available in…

3. *Bible Dictionary*
    a. Provides the following information

        1)

        2)

       3)

       4)

       5)

       6)

4. *Topical Concordance*
   a. Differs from a regular concordance in...

   b. Provides the following information
      1)

      2)

      3)

5. *Pronouncing Bible Names*
   a. Provides the following information
      1)

      2)

      3)

6. *Study Bible*
   a. Provides the following information
      1)

      2)

      3)

4)

5)

6)

7. *Bible Handbook*
   a. Provides the following information
   1)

   2)

   3)

   4)

   5)

   6)

8. *One-Volume Commentary*
   a. Provides the following information
   1)

   2)

   3)

   4)

   5)

   6)

9. *Introduction to Old (New) Testament*
   a. Provides the following information
      I)

      2)

      3)

      4)

      5)

      6)

10. *History of Israel/of New Testament Times*
   a. Provides the following information
      1)

      2)

      3)

      4)

      5)

      6)

11. *Gospels Paralleled*
   a. Provides the following information
      1)

      2)

      3)

4)

5)

6)

Take one or more of the following questions and find answers to them in one or more of the reference books named above.

1. When and why was the gospel of Luke written?

2. How many times does the gospel of Luke use the term "kingdom of God"?

3. What is the meaning of the term "kingdom of God" in the gospels?

4. Does the same Greek word underlie all the occurrences of the word "love" in Luke's gospel?

5. What does Luke's gospel say about the poor?

6. What other gospel writers tell the story of the raising of the son of a widow of Nain found in Luke 7:11–17?

7. What differences occur in Matthew and Luke's version of the healing of the centurion's servant found in Matthew 8:5–13 and Luke 7:1–10?

8. What are possible interpretations of the "unforgivable sin" in Luke 12:10?

9. List the birds and animals that appear in the Bible.

10. What are the major problems in dating the exodus of Israel from Egypt?

11. What passage from Isaiah is John the Baptist quoting in Luke 3:4–6?

The Nature of the New Testament

Time Periods

- Gospel Events 6 B.C.E. to 29 (31) C.E.
- Acts Events and writing of James 29 (31) to 63 C.E.
- Paul's Ministry 32 to 63 C.E. (64–68: Pastoral Epistles)
- Temple Destroyed 70 C.E.
- Other New Testament Writings 70 to 96

The Old Testament Books as Background

Jewish Divisions

- Law
- Prophets
- Former Prophets (Joshua, Judges, Samuel, Kings)
- Latter Prophets (Isaiah, Jeremiah, Ezekiel, the Twelve Minor Prophets [as one book])
- Writings (Psalms, Job, Proverbs, Ruth, Song of Songs, Ecclesiastes, Lamentations, Esther, Daniel, Ezra/Nehemiah, Chronicles)

Christian Divisions

- Pentateuch
- History (Joshua, Judges, Ruth, Samuel, 1 Kings, 2 Kings, 1 Chronicles, 2 Chronicles, Ezra, Nehemiah, Esther)
- Poetry (Job, Psalms, Proverbs, Ecclesiastes, Song of Solomon)
- Prophets (Isaiah, Jeremiah, Lamentations, Ezekiel, Daniel, the Twelve Minor Prophets [as separate books])
- Apocrypha (1 Esdras, 2 Esdras, Tobit, Judith, The Additions to the Book of Esther, The Wisdom of Solomon, Ecclesiasticus, or the Wisdom of Jesus the Son of Sirach, Baruch, The Letter of Jeremiah, The Prayer of Azariah and the Song of the Three Young Men, Susanna, Bel and the Dragon, The Prayer of Manasseh, 1 Maccabees, 2 Maccabees

Septuagint

(Early Greek translation from about 250 to 50 b.c.e. often quoted in NT and used in the early church)

- Law
- History (Joshua, Judges, Ruth, 4 Books of Kings, Chronicles, 1 Esdras, 2 Esdras=Ezra/Nehemiah, Esther with additions, Judith, Tobit, 4 Books of Maccabees
- Poetry (Psalms with Psalm 151, Odes, Proverbs, Ecclesiastes, Song of Songs, Job, Wisdom of Solomon, Sirach or Ecclesiasticus, Psalms of Solomon
- Prophets (Hosea, Amos, Micah, Joel, Obadiah, Jonah, Nahum, Habakkuk, Zephaniah, Haggai, Zechariah, Malachi, Isaiah, Jeremiah (which is 12 percent shorter than Hebrew text, omitting passages such as 33:14–26 and 39:4–13 and placing chapters 46—51 after 25:13, but also contains Baruch, Lamentations, and the Epistle of Jeremiah), Ezekiel, and Daniel (including Susanna sometimes placed before chapter 1, Bel and the Dragon, and The Prayer of Azariah and the Hymn of the Three Young Men placed between 3:23 and 3:24)

A Brief History of English Bible Translations

English Versions of the Bible

1. Caedmon, monk about 670 C.E.—metrical translation of parts of Bible

2. Bede about 700 translated gospels into Anglo-Saxon

3. Guthlac about 700 made English glosses on Latin texts of Psalms; several other such glossed texts

4. Aldhelm, about 700, abbot of Malmesburay translated Psalms into Anglo-Saxon

5. Egbert about 700 translated gospels

6. West Saxon Gospels about 1000

7. Aelfric about 1000 abridged and translated Genesis through Judges

8. Orm about 1200 used gospels as basis of paraphrase

9. West Midland Psalter about 1350

10. Northern metrical version about 1300

11. Richard Rolle about 1325 translated Psalms into English

12. South England had translations of Peter; James; 1,2,3 John; Paul's letters about 1325

13. John Wycliffe made English translation about 1382

14. John Purvey in 1388 revised Wycliffe

15. 1408 Council in Oxford said bishop had to approve any translation

16. William Caxton in 1483 produced *The Golden Legend,* including books of Moses, some of historical books, and paraphrase of the gospels

17. William Tyndale produced printed New Testament in 1525 in Hamburg, but Henry VIII made this translation illegal to read

18. About 1530 Tyndale issued Pentateuch and Psalms; Jonah came in 1531; Joshua to 2 Chronicles in 1536 just before his execution

19. George Joye about 1530 did Psalms, Isaiah, part of Genesis, Proverbs through Lamentations

20. 1537 saw royal licenses for printing of Coverdale's Bible (by assistant of Tyndale) and Matthew's Bible called the Great Bible (by Thomas Matthews, whose real name was John Rogers, another friend of Tyndale); 1539 saw Richard Taverner's Bible printed, first Bible totally printed in England

21. By 1546 Tyndale's and Coverdale's Bibles were prohibited

22. In 1570 Geneva Bible was translated by William Whittingham. This was the Bible used early by King James, by Shakespeare, by John Bunyan, the Puritans, and the Pilgrims

23. Matthew Parker used bishops of the church to produce the Bishops' Bible in 1568

24. Gregory Martin, William Allen and Richard Baristow worked at Rheims in France and produced the Rheims-Douay Bible in 1582, official Roman Catholic translation for centuries.

25. *King James Bible* published in 1611 with Apocrypha (as all previous English Bibles), based on Bishops' Bible while consulting others; had financial problems raising funds for project; first revision came in 1616.

Early Modern English Translations

1871 The *New Translation* by John Nelson Darby of Plymouth Brethren

1885 *English Revised Version* by government committee

1901 American version of 1885 edition called *American Standard Version*

1902 *Twentieth Century New Testament*

1903 *The New Testament in Modern Speech* by Richard Weymouth

1913 *The New Testament: A New Translation* by James Moffatt; Old Testament, 1926

1931 *The Complete Bible: An American Translation* by Edgar J. Goodspeed and J. M. Powis Smith

1952 *Revised Standard Version* by World Council of Churches Committee

1970 *New English Bible*, official British revision,

1976 *Good News Bible: Today's English Version,* by American Bible Society

Critical Analysis of Some Recent Bible Translations

New American Standard Bible, 1971; slight revision in 1995

> 1. Retains traditional language always: gospel, resurrection, grace, spiritual gift, covenant, righteousness, reconciliation, trespasses, etc.
>
> 2. Maintains ambiguity of original language without additional interpretation (does make theological decision using propitiation)
>
> 3. Maintains biblical figures of speech: sting of death, fallen asleep, thorn in the flesh

God's Word, 1995

> 1. Replaces all traditional language:
>
> *flesh*: human nature; corrupt nature
>
> *resurrection*: came back to life
>
> *grace*: kindness or good will or favor
>
> *spiritual gift*: spiritual blessing
>
> *righteousness*: God's approval; God is fair
>
> *justified*: God's approval
>
> *fear of God*: terrified of God
>
> *glory*: honor from God
>
> *redemption*: price Jesus paid to set us free from sin; ransom from sin
>
> *Law*: his own efforts, rules; God's standards
>
> *transgressions*: failures
>
> *hope*: confidence
>
> *reconciliation*: friendship with God
>
> *eternal life*: living forever
>
> *confession*: declaring your faith
>
> *covenants*: pledges, promises, arrangements
>
> *salvation*: you are saved

tongue: another language

trespasses: people's faults

repentance: change the way they think and act

2. Generally maintains ambiguity of original language but word choices often weaken original meanings

3. Usually gives literal figures of speech but not always: sting

New Revised Standard Version, 1989

1. Retains traditional language always: gospel, resurrection, grace, spiritual gift, covenant, righteousness, reconciliation, trespasses, etc.

   In Rom. 6:19 "flesh" becomes "natural limitations"

2. Maintains ambiguity of original language without additional interpretation (RSV makes theological decision using "expiation," changed in NRSV to "sacrifice of atonement")

3. Maintains biblical figures of speech: sting of death, fallen asleep, thorn in the flesh

   NRSV changes "fallen asleep" to "died in Christ"

Revised English Bible, 1989

1. Retains traditional language for the most part: gospel, resurrection, grace, spiritual gift, covenant, righteousness, reconciliation, trespasses, etc.

   flesh: on human level, your human weakness, our sinful nature

   grace: "the privilege of" in Rom. 1:5

   fear of God: reverence for God

   redemption: liberation

   transgressions: misdeeds

   repentance: change of heart

2. Maintains ambiguity of original language without additional interpretation (does make theological decision to keep means of expiating sin)

3. Maintains biblical figures of speech: sting of death, fallen asleep, thorn in the flesh

   fallen asleep in Christ: died within Christ's fellowship

Contemporary English Version, 1995

1. Changes almost all traditional language to contemporary idiom:

   gospel: good news

   flesh: as a human, in some ways you are still weak, be like us sinners

   grace: kind, undeserved kindness

   spiritual gift: blessings

   righteousness of God: how God accepts, how right God is, become acceptable to God

   justified: treats us much better than we deserve

   redemption: freely accepts us and sets us free from our sins, acceptable, rescues

   propitiation/expiation: our sacrifice

   transgressions: sins

   *reconciliatio*n: make peace with us

   resurrection: will be raised to life

   covenants: agreements

   confession: tell it to others

   tongues: languages that others don't know

   repentance: turn to him

2. Maintains ambiguity of original language without additional interpretation

3. Translates most biblical figures of speech into modern idiom

4. Tends at times to omit biblical terms and at other times to add explanatory words

The Message, 2002

1. Does not attempt any word-for-word translation, but rather becomes expansive, interpretative, and explanatory in almost every verse. Uses no verse numbers. Many scholars catalog this Bible as a paraphrase, not as a translation.

2. Apparently takes contemporary audience so into consideration that it avoids terms for specific sins, such as adultery and homosexuality, etc.

3. Does maintain some traditional vocabulary such as Spirit, Law, covenant, sin, redeemed—but inconsistently

4. Sample word transformations show some translation techniques:

good news: God's words and acts

flesh: descent in history, human condition, the disordered mess of struggling humanity

resurrection: was raised from the dead

grace: generous, generosity, enjoy the best of Jesus

righteousness: God's way of putting people right, live right before God

justified: what makes the difference with God, put us in right standing

righteousness: God's rightdoing

fear of God: give God the time of day

glory of God: glorious lives God wills for us

redemption: got us out of the mess we're in and restored us to where he always wanted us to be, a fresh start

reconciliation: amazing friendship, settled the relationship, put the world square with himself

eternal life: life that goes on and on and on world without end

believe: embrace God with your whole being

confess: say it out loud: "God has set everything right between him and me"

tongue: private language of tongues

repentance: turns us around, gets us back in the way of salvation

thorn in the flesh: gift of a handicap

law: keeping rules and working my head off

covenant: two ways of being in relationship with God

5. Major characteristic is addition of entire sentences and of explanatory phrases and clauses that lead to extremely long sentences.

NIrV: *New International Reader's Version,* 1998

1. Retains traditional language (Holy Spirit, grace, glory, law, eternal life, covenants) in many, even unexpected, cases for children

2. Has consistent translation changes for key terms

gospel: good news

flesh: human being, human, sinful nature

resurrection: rose from the dead

spiritual gift: gift from the Holy Spirit

righteousness: how God makes people right with him; God is right

justified: considered to be right with God

fear of God: respect for God

redemption: paid the price to set us free, sets us free

reconciliation: God has brought us back to himself

confess: say that Jesus is Lord

tongues: languages they had not known

3. Generally gives conservative theological interpretation of ambiguous passages

4. Generally does not maintains biblical figures of speech, putting them in modern idiom

5. Major characteristic is extremely short sentences, leading generally to several sentences in each verse and more words in each verse.

New Century Version, 1991

1. Retains much traditional language (grace, fear of God, Holy Spirit, spiritual gift, glory, law, sins)

2. Has consistent translation changes for key terms

gospel: good news

flesh: as a man

resurrection: rise from the dead

grace: special work (exceptional case; often uses grace)

righteousness of God: how God makes people right with himself; God is right

justified: make people right with God

redemption: made free from sin

reconciliation: God's friends again, made peace between us and himself, took away the curse, changed places with us

eternal life: life forever

sinful flesh: with the same human life that others use for sin

covenants: agreements

confess: use our mouths to say we believe

tongue: different languages

repentance: change their hearts and lives

3. Generally retains ambiguity of original text without interpretation

4. Usually translates figures of speech into modern idiom

5. Does not always follow the sentence structure and grammatical constructions of the original

The Living Bible, 1971

1. Major characteristic: deviates considerably from original texts, even adding and omitting materials.

2. Original translation included a spattering of four-letter words in Samuel

3. One person's interpretation of Scripture

4. Simplifies vocabulary:

gospel: Good News

flesh: as a man

resurrection: powerfully raised him from the dead

grace: special work, God's mercies, gracious kindness, place of highest privilege, wonderful kindness

spiritual gift: spiritual blessing

righteousness of God: how God makes people right in his sight; how good God is

justified: declared right in God's sight, declares us not guilty

fear of God: reverence for God

glory of God: God's glorious ideal

redemption: free us by taking away our sins, purchase our salvation

propitiation: to take the punishment for our sins and to satisfy God's anger

works of the law: good things we do

reconciliation: making us friends of God, brought us back to himself, restoring the world to himself

eternal life: life forever

sinful flesh: in a human body like ours—except that ours are sinful

> *confess*: call upon the name of the Lord
>
> *tongue*: "speak in tongues," that is, speak in languages you haven't learned
>
> *repentance*: turn away from sin and seek eternal life

New International Version, 1984

1. Retains traditional language in most cases: gospel, resurrection, grace, spiritual gift, covenant, righteousness, reconciliation, trespasses, etc.

2. Provides conservative theological interpretation in most cases, with specific theological guidelines, particularly in case of quotations from Old Testament and references to Sheol in Old Testament

3. Maintains biblical figures of speech: sting of death, fallen asleep, thorn in the flesh

The New Living Translation, 1996, 2004

1. Update of *The Living Translation* by modern scholars trying to give it place as acceptable academic translation.

2. Still very free in translation, omitting phrases, and bringing figures of speech up to date.

3. Good for introducing people to Bible reading or for one who wants to read the Bible through in a new translation

Holman Christian Standard Bible, 2004

1. Seeks midway translation point between literalness of NASB and dynamic equivalent NIV

2. Maintains traditional language in most places

3. Updates some figures of speech

4. Capitalizes pronouns and other words referring to God

English Standard Version, 2001

> Slight update of original *Revised Standard Version* by evangelical scholars.

Selection of Translation Problems

There are some common verses, the translations of which are often disputed, yet they are vital to theology and christology. I have included several examples of these verses and show how each is translated in various Bible versions.

Genesis 1:1–2—Here the key differences in renderings arise from the translation of *ruach elohim*. *Ruach* in Hebrew can mean "wind" or "breath"—or "spirit" in the case of a rational being. Here the translators are at liberty to choose which one they feel is best. Spirit of God is probably the most traditional. The Church Fathers often saw the trinitarian connection in creation: the Father creates through the Logos (Word), while the Spirit hovered over the waters. The NAB translates the verse using *elohim* as descriptive of the wind. In Hebrew, something "of God" could also mean the best, most powerful, or strongest of the thing being described.

Isaiah 7:14—The difference here is over the translation of the Hebrew word *almah*. The Hebrew word means not just a virgin, but any young woman. The Greek word used in the Septuagint translation for *almah*, however, means virgin in the strictest sense (*parthenos*). Some scholars say that the prophecy probably originally was about a young woman, the birth of whose son would signify that God was with his people. However, the author of Matthew sees in this verse a prophecy about the virgin birth of Christ, the ultimate fulfillment of "God with us" in the incarnate Son. Thus, this verse could have a double fulfillment: the shorter term and the longer term. "Virgin" is the most traditional translation (cf. the LXX, Vulgate, and KJV), but "young woman" is probably most faithful to the Hebrew.

John 1:1—Here is a verse that is somewhat controversial, thanks mainly to the Jehovah's Witnesses. They make a big deal of the Greek construction. *Theos* (Greek for God) has an article (*ho*) when used the first time, but lacks it the second time. They conclude that lacking the article means that the word was not the Almighty God, but simply *a* god. In English it's best to put the verse like this: "In the beginning was the Word, the Word was with (the) God, and the Word was God." The lacking article merely describes the nature of the Word. John 1:1 does not tell us who the Word is, but *how* the Word is. This is best seen in Kenneth Wuest's *The New Testament: An Expanded Translation*, "In the beginning the Word was existing. And the Word was in fellowship with God the Father And the Word was as to His essence absolute deity," or the REB, "[W]hat God was, the Word was." The construction notes Christ is not *the* God (the title John apparently reserves for the Father), but God by nature. Thus, Christ is God the Son. This fits with 1:18, which states that no one has seen God, but God the One and Only (or God the Only Son) has declared him. John chose his words carefully. If he identified the Logos with *the* God, he would not have distinguished the Word from the God he is with, a later view known as modalism or Sabellianism. As it stands, John 1:1, far from being anti-Trinitarian (or binarian in this case) is quite so.

John 1:18—The majority of manuscripts of the gospel of John have *monogenes huios,* which means "Only Begotten Son" or "One and Only Son." But the best texts of John read *monogenes theos.* Origen and Clement of Alexandria also testify to this reading. This calls Christ the "Only Begotten God," or "One and Only God." Some translators see *monogenes* as not only unique but filial, and translate it "Only Son," as does the NRSV, which has "God the Only Son." This is another very Trinitarian (or in this case binarian) verse, which reveals one God, yet two persons within the Godhead.

Romans 9:5—The Greek language lacked punctuation, and some verses can be translated differently by using different punctuation. Here is a literal translation with no punctuation: "…of whom the fathers and from whom the Christ accord (ing) flesh the being over all God blessed unto the ages." Some put a period or colon after "flesh." If translated like the NRSV, NIV, NASB, NJB, or Wuest, it argues for Christ's divinity, otherwise (NAB, NWT, TEV, REB) it does not. Nearly all Church Fathers from the earliest times until the Middle Ages regarded this verse as an example of Christ's divinity, but other later, respected scholars did not (e.g., Erasmus).

Colossians 2:9—The important word here is *theotes.* The word means literally "Godship," "Godhood," or "Deity." The word is abstract, denoting a quality: the quality of being God. The NWT reads "divine quality," which tries to water down the verse, and is a biased and incorrect rendering. Also, the term "Godhead" (KJV, ASV, REB) can be slightly misleading. Godhead (a term rarely heard outside of Christianity by most Christians) has the general meaning of "deity." Thus, this verse in no way implies Christ is each person in the Godhead (modalism), but that he possesses each and every trait of the Godhead.

Titus 2:13—The question here is whether one person is being referred to—that is, Christ (as both God and Savior)—or two, God and the Savior Christ. The Greek language strongly points to one person being referred to.

Revelation 3:14—The word used here, *arche,* means beginning, but not in the sense of the created. It is used in John 1:1 to show the eternality of Christ, for example ("In the beginning…"). Many agree that it is best translated as "origin" or "source." Thus the beginning means the one who begins to do. For example, if I sculpt something out of clay, I am the beginning of the sculpture. Why? I'm creating it; I'm the source of the art, the shape, and the sculpture. Christ is the beginning of God's creation, the Creator, the Origin, the Principle, etc.

And Now the Verses in Different Translations

ASV

1. In the beginning God created the heavens and the earth. And the earth was waste and void; and darkness was upon the face of the deep: and the Spirit of God moved upon the face of the waters.

2. Therefore the Lord himself will give you a sign: behold, a virgin shall conceive, and bear a son, and shall call his name Immanuel.

3. In the beginning was the Word, and the Word was with God, and the Word was God

4. No man hath seen God at any time; the only begotten Son, who is in the bosom of the Father, he hath declared him.

5. …whose are the fathers, and of whom is Christ as concerning the flesh, who is over all, God blessed forever. Amen.

6. …for in him dwelleth all the fulness of the Godhead bodily…

7. …looking for the blessed hope and appearing of the glory of the great God and our Saviour Jesus Christ

8. And to the angel of the church in Laodicea write: These things saith the Amen, the faithful and true witness, the beginning of the creation of God

Douay-Reims

1. In the beginning God created heaven, and earth. And the earth was void and empty, and darkness was upon the face of the deep; and the spirit of God moved over the waters.

2. Therefore the Lord himself shall give you a sign. Behold a virgin shall conceive, and bear a son, and his name shall be called Emmanuel.

3. In the beginning was the Word, and the Word was with God, and the Word was God.

4. No man hath seen God at any time: the only begotten Son who is in the bosom of the Father, he hath declared him.

5. Whose are the fathers, and of whom is Christ, according to the flesh, who is over all things, God blessed for ever. Amen.

6. For in him dwelleth all the fulness of the Godhead corporeally;

7. Looking for the blessed hope and coming of the glory of the great God and our Savior Jesus Christ

8. And to the angel of the church of Laodicea, write: These things saith the Amen, the faithful and true witness, who is the beginning of the creation of God.

KJV

1. In the beginning God created the heaven and the earth. And the earth was without form, and void; and darkness was upon the face of the deep. And the Spirit of God moved upon the face of the waters.

2. Therefore the Lord himself shall give you a sign; Behold, a virgin shall conceive, and bear a son, and shall call his name Immanuel.

3. In the beginning was the Word, and the Word was with God, and the Word was God.

4. No man hath seen God at any time; the only begotten Son, which is in the bosom of the Father, he hath declared him.

5. Whose are the fathers, and of whom as concerning the flesh Christ came, who is over all, God blessed forever. Amen.

6. For in him dwelleth all the fullness of the Godhead bodily.

7. Looking for that blessed hope, and the glorious appearing of the great God and our Saviour Jesus Christ;

8. And unto the angel of the church of the Laodiceans write; These things saith the Amen, the faithful and true witness, the beginning of the creation of God;

LB

1. When God began creating the heavens and the earth, the earth was a shapeless, chaotic mass, with the Spirit of God brooding over the dark vapors.

2. All right then, the Lord himself will choose the sign—a child shall be born to a virgin! And she shall call him Immanuel (meaning, "God is with us").

3. Before anything else existed, there was Christ, with God. He has always been alive and is himself God.

4. No one has ever actually seen God, but, of course, his only Son has, for he is the companion of the Father and has told us all about him.

5. Great men of God were your fathers, and Christ himself was one of you, a Jew so far as his human nature is concerned, he who now rules over all things. Praise God forever!

6. For in Christ there is all of God in a human body;

7. ...looking forward to that wonderful time we've been expecting, when his glory shall be seen—the glory of our great God and Savior Jesus Christ.

8. Write this letter to the leader of the church in Laodicea: 'This message is from the one who stands firm, the faithful and true Witness [of all that is or was or evermore shall be], the primeval source of God's creation:

James Moffatt

1. When God began to form the universe, the world was void and vacant, darkness lay over the abyss; but the spirit of God was hovering over the waters.

2. An omen you shall have, and that from the Eternal himself. There is a young woman with a child who shall bear a son and call his name Immanuel

3. The Logos existed in the very beginning, the Logos was with God, the Logos was divine.

4. Nobody has ever seen God, but God has been unfolded by the divine One, the Only Son, who lies upon the Father's breast.

5. the patriarchs are theirs, and theirs too (so far as natural descent goes) is the Christ. (Blessed be forever more the God who is over all! Amen.)

6. It is in Christ that the entire fulness of deity has settled bodily.

7. ...awaiting the blessed hope of the appearance of the Glory of the great God and of our savior Christ Jesus...

8. Then to the angel of the church in Laodicea, write this: These are the words of The Amen, the faithful and true witness, the origin of God's creation.

NAB

1. In the beginning, when God created the heavens and the earth, the earth was a formless wasteland, and darkness covered the abyss, while a mighty wind swept over the waters.

2. Therefore the Lord himself will give you this sign: the virgin shall be with child, and bear a son, and shall name him Immanuel.

3. In the beginning was the Word, and the Word was with God, and the Word was God.

4. No one has ever seen God. The only Son, God, who is at the Father's side, has revealed him.

5. Theirs the patriarchs, and from them, according to the flesh, is the Messiah. God who is over all be blessed forever. Amen.

6. For in him dwells the whole fullness of the deity bodily,

7. As we await the blessed hope, the appearance of the glory of the great God and of our savior Jesus Christ,

8. "To the angel of the church in Laodicea, write this: 'The Amen, the faithful and true witness, the source of God's creation, says this:

NASB95

1. In the beginning God created the heavens and the earth. The earth was formless and void, and darkness was over the surface of the deep, and the Spirit of God was moving over the surface of the waters.

2. "Therefore the Lord Himself will give you a sign: Behold, a virgin will be with child and bear a son, and she will call His name Immanuel.

3. In the beginning was the Word, and the Word was with God, and the Word was God.

4. No one has seen God at any time; the only begotten God, who is in the bosom of the Father, He has explained Him.

5. …whose are the fathers, and from whom is the Christ according to the flesh, who is over all, God blessed forever. Amen.

6. For in Him all the fullness of Deity dwells in bodily form

7. …looking for the blessed hope and the appearing of the glory of our great God and Savior, Christ Jesus;

8. "To the angel of the church in Laodicea write: The Amen, the faithful and true Witness, the Beginning of the creation of God, says this:

NET

1. In the beginning God created the entire universe. Now the earth was without shape and empty, and darkness was over the surface of the watery deep; but the Spirit of God was moving over the surface of the water.

2. For this reason the sovereign master himself will give you a confirming sign. Look, the young lady over there is about to conceive and will give birth to a son. You, young lady, will name him Immanuel.

3. In the beginning was the Word, and the Word was with God, and the Word was God.

4. No one has ever seen God. The only One, himself God, who is in the presence of the Father, has made God known.

5. To them belong the patriarchs, and from them, by human descent, came the Christ, who is God over all, blessed forever! Amen.

6. For in him all the fullness of deity lives in bodily form.

7. ...as we wait for the happy fulfillment of our hope in the glorious appearing of our great God and Savior, Jesus Christ.

8. This is the solemn pronouncement of the Amen, the faithful and true witness, the originator of God's creation:

NIV

1. In the beginning God created the heavens and the earth. Now the earth was formless and empty, darkness was over the surface of the deep, and the Spirit of God was hovering over the waters.

2. Therefore the Lord himself will give you a sign: The virgin will be with child and will give birth to a son, and will call him Immanuel.

3. In the beginning was the Word, and the Word was with God, and the Word was God.

4. No one has ever seen God, but God the only Son, who is at the Father's side, has made him known.

5. Theirs are the patriarchs, and from them is traced the human ancestry of Christ, who is God over all, forever praised! Amen.

6. For in Christ all the fullness of the Deity lives in bodily form,

7. ...while we wait for the blessed hope—the glorious appearing of our great God and Savior, Jesus Christ,

8. "To the angel of the church in Laodicea write: These are the words of the Amen, the faithful and true witness, the ruler of God's creation..."

NJB

1. In the beginning God created heaven and earth. Now the earth was a formless void, there was darkness over the deep, with a divine wind sweeping over the waters.

2. The Lord will give you a sign in any case: It is this: the young woman is with child and will give birth to a son whom she will call Immanuel.

3. In the beginning was the Word: the Word was with God and the Word was God.

4. No one has ever seen God; it is the only Son, who is close to the Father's heart, who has made him known.

5. To them belong the fathers and out of them, so far as physical descent is concerned, came Christ who is above all, God, blessed forever. Amen.

6. In him, in bodily form, lives divinity in all its fullness,

7. ...waiting in hope for the blessing which will come with the appearing of the glory of our great God and Saviour Christ Jesus

8. "Write to the angel of the church in Laodicea and say, 'Here is the message of the Amen, the trustworthy, the true witness, the Principle of God's creation:

NKJV

1. In the beginning God created the heavens and the earth. The earth was without form, and void; and darkness was on the face of the deep. And the Spirit of God was hovering over the face of the waters.

2. "Therefore the Lord Himself will give you a sign: Behold, the virgin shall conceive and bear a Son, and shall call His name Immanuel.

3. In the beginning was the Word, and the Word was with God, and the Word was God.

4. No one has seen God at any time. The only begotten Son, who is in the bosom of the Father, He has declared Him.

5. ...of whom are the fathers and from whom, according to the flesh, Christ came, who is over all, the eternally blessed God. Amen.

6. For in Him dwells all the fullness of the Godhead bodily;

7. ...looking for the blessed hope and glorious appearing of our great God and Savior Jesus Christ,

8. "And to the angel of the church of the Laodiceans write, 'These things says the Amen, the Faithful and True Witness, the Beginning of the creation of God:...'"

NRSV

1. In the beginning when God created the heavens and the earth, the earth was a formless void and darkness covered the face of the deep, while a wind from God swept over the face of the waters.

2. Therefore the Lord himself will give you a sign. Look, the young woman is with child and shall bear a son, and shall name him Immanuel.

3. In the beginning was the Word, and the Word was with God, and the Word was God.

4. No one has ever seen God. It is God the only Son, who is close to the Father's heart, who has made him known.

5. ...to them belong the patriarchs, and from them, according to the flesh, comes the Messiah, who is over all, God blessed forever. Amen.

6. For in him the whole fullness of deity dwells bodily...

7. ...while we wait for the blessed hope and the manifestation of the glory of our great God and Savior, Jesus Christ.

8. "And to the angel of the church in Laodicea write: The words of the Amen, the faithful and true witness, the origin of God's creation:..."

NWT

1. In the beginning God created the heavens and the earth. Now the earth proved to be formless and waste and there was darkness upon the surface of the watery deep; and God's active force was moving to and fro over the surface of the waters

2. Therefore Jehovah himself will give you a sign will give you men a sign: Look! The maiden herself will actually become pregnant and she is giving birth to a son, and she will certainly call his name Immanuel

3. In the beginning the Word was, and the Word was with God, and the Word was a god

4. No man has seen God at any time; the only begotten god who is in the bosom [position] with the Father, has declared him

5. To whom the forefathers belong and from whom the Christ sprang according to the flesh: God, who is over all blessed forever. Amen

6. For it is in him that all the fullness of the divine quality dwells bodily

7. While we wait for the happy hope and glorious manifestation of the great God and of the Savior of us, Christ Jesus

8. And to the angel in the congregation of Laodicea write: These are the things that the Amen says, the faithful and true witness, the beginning of the creation by God.

REB

1. In the beginning God created the heavens and the earth. The earth was a vast waste, darkness covered the deep, and the spirit of God hovered over the surface of the water.

2. Because you do, the Lord of his own accord will give you a sign; it is this: A young woman is with child and she will give birth to a son, and call him Immanuel.

3. In the beginning the Word already was. The Word was in God's presence, and what God was, the Word was.

4. No one has ever seen God; God's only Son, he who is nearest to the Father's heart, has made him known.

5. The patriarchs are theirs, and from them by natural descent came the Messiah. May God, supreme above all, be blessed forever! Amen.

6. For it is in Christ that the Godhead in all its fullness dwells embodied.

7. …looking forward to the happy fulfillment of our hope when the splendor of our great God and Savior, Christ Jesus will appear.

8. To the angel in the church of Laodicia write: "These are the words of the Amen, the faithful and true witness, the source of God's creation.

TEV

1. In the beginning when God created the universe, the earth was formless and desolate. The raging ocean that covered everything was engulfed in total darkness, and the Spirit of God was moving over the water

2. Well then, the Lord himself will give you a sign: a young woman who is pregnant will have a son and will name him Immanuel

3. In the beginning the Word already existed; the Word was with God, and the Word was God

4. No one has ever seen God. The only Son, who is the same as God and is at the Father's side, he has made him known.

5. …they are descended from the famous Hebrew ancestors; and Christ as a human being, belongs to their race. May God, who rules over all, be praised forever! Amen.

6. For the full content of divine nature lives in Christ, in his humanity…

7. …as we wait for the blessed Day we hope for, when the glory of our great God and Savior Jesus Christ will appear.

8. "To the angel of the church in Laodicea write: 'This is the message from the Amen, the faithful and true witness, who is the origin of all that God has created…'"

WUEST

1. N/A
2. N/A
3. In the beginning the Word was existing. And the Word was in fellowship with God the Father, and the Word was as to His essence absolute deity.
4. Absolute deity in its essence no one has ever yet seen. God uniquely begotten, he who is in the bosom of the Father, that One fully explained deity.
5. ...of whom are the fathers, and out from whom is the Christ according to the flesh, The One who is above all, God eulogized forever. Amen.
6. ...because in him there is continuously and permanently at home all the fullness of absolute deity in bodily fashion.
7. ...expectantly looking for the prosperous expectation, even the appearing of the glory of our great God and Saviour Jesus Christ.
8. And to the messenger of the assembly in Laodicea write at once: These things say the Amen, the witness who is trustworthy and dependable, the originating source of the creation of God.

Basic Bible Study Resources

Bible Dictionary

Holman Illustrated Bible Dictionary, 1991, rev. 2003, ed. Trent C. Butler

The Anchor Bible Dictionary, Doubleday, 1992, David Noel Freedman

Evangelical Dictionary of Biblical Theology, Baker, 2001, ed. Walter A. Elwell

Harper Collins Bible Dictionary, Society of Biblical Literature, 1996, ed. Paul Achtemeier

The New Interpreter's Dictionary of the Bible, Abingdon Press, 2009, ed. Katherine Doob Sakenfeld

Bible Concordance

Complete concordance has all significant words, with omissions of secondary words.

Exhaustive concordance lists every word and occurrence in Bible.

Concordances are keyed to specific translations, so get the concordance keyed to translation you use most for Bible study.

Bible Handbook

Holman Bible Handbook, 1992, ed. David Dockery

The New Jerome Bible Handbook, Liturgical, 1992, ed. Roland Edmund Murphy

Bible Atlas

Holman Bible Atlas, 1998, Thomas Brisco

The Sacred Bridge, Carta, 2005, ed. Anson Rainey

Study Bible
(get one keyed to the translation you use most often, and one in a different translation)

Basic Bible Information

NIV Study Bible, Zondervan, 1985, rev. 2008

The NET Bible, Biblical Studies Press, 2001

NKJV Study Bible, Thomas Nelson, 2008

The New Oxford Annotated Bible, Oxford, 2008

Devotional, Personal Growth

Experiencing God Study Bible, Henry Blackaby, 1996

Theological Study Bible

Disciples Study Bible, Holman, 1988, ed. Trent C. Butler

Dispensational Theology
Ryrie Study Bible, Baker, 1976, ed. Charles Ryrie, available for different Bible versions

Life Application
Life Application Study Bible, Tyndale, available for different Bible versions

Gospels Paralleled

Synopsis of the Four Gospels, United Bible Societies, 1982, ed. Kurt Aland
A Simplified Harmony of the Gospels, Holman, 2001, George Knight
The Complete Parallel Bible, Oxford, 1993

Introduction to the Old Testament

Chalice Introduction to the Old Testament, Chalice, 2003, ed. Marti J. Steussy
Old Testament Survey, 2d ed. B&H Academic, 2007, Paul House and Eric Mitchell
An Introduction to the Old Testament, Zondervan, 2006, Raymond Dillard and Tremper Longman III
Encountering the Old Testament, Baker, 2008, Bryan E. Beyer and Bill T. Arnold
An Introduction to the Old Testament, Westminster John Knox, 2003, Walter Brueggemann

Introduction to the New Testament

Chalice Introduction to the New Testament, Chalice, 2004, ed. Dennis E. Smith
The New Testament: Its Background and Message, Broadman & Holman, 2003, Thomas D. Lea and David Allen Black
An Introduction to the New Testament: Contexts, Methods & Ministry Formation, InterVarsity, 2003, David A. DeSilva
An Introduction to the New Testament, Zondervan, 1992, D. A. Carson, Douglas J. Moo, and Leon Morris
Introducing the New Testament, Baker Academic, 2009, M. A. Powell

History of Israel

A History of Israel, Broadman and Holman, 1998, Walter C. Kaiser Jr.
A Biblical History of Israel, Westminster John Knox, 2003, Iain Provan, V. Philips Long, Tremper Longman III—for advanced students
An Introduction to the Old Testament Pentateuch, Moody, 2007, Herbert Wolf
An Introduction to the Old Testament Historical Books, Moody, 1993, David M. Howard Jr.

An Introduction to the Old Testament Poetic Books, Moody, 1988, C. Hassell Bullock

An Introduction to the Old Testament Prophetic Books, Moody, 1986, C. Hassell Bullock

Commentaries—Series
*(suitable for lay-people; one volume if possible, up-to-date;
not available for all books)*

Holman Old Testament Commentary, ed. Max Anders, for lay teachers (HOTC)

Holman New Testament Commentary, ed. Max Anders, for lay teachers (HNTC)

New American Commentary, Broadman and Holman, advanced (NAC)

NIV Life Application Commentary, Zondervan, advanced (LAC)

Interpretation, Westminster/John Knox, critical, for preaching (INT)

Tyndale Old (New) Testament Commentaries, Tyndale, good for laity (TOTC) (TNTC)

New International Commentary on the Old (New) Testament, Eerdmans, advanced (NICOT) (NICNT)

Word Biblical Commentary, Thomas Nelson/Word, for advanced students (WBC)

Expositor's Bible Commentary, Zondervan, 12 Volumes (EBC)

New International Biblical Commentary, Hendrickson (NIBC)

New Century Bible, critical (NCB)

Old Testament Library, Westminster/John Knox, very critical (OTL)

Wycliffe Exegetical Commentary, Moody (WEC)

Readings: A New Biblical Commentary (classical reprints and new literary, psychological readings), Sheffield Phoenix Press (Readings)

Apollos Old Testament Commentary, IVP (Apollos)

Sacra Pagina, a multi-volume commentary (Liturgical Press)

Smyth and Helwys Bible Commentary, Smyth and Helwys, done for preachers; includes CD-Rom (S&H)

New Interpreter's Bible, Abingdon, critical with homiletic exposition (NIB)

Anchor Bible, Doubleday, critical and detailed but quite uneven (AB)

New International Greek Testament Commentary, advanced (NIGTC)

Commentaries—Books

Genesis—Walter Brueggemann, Int; Ken Matthews, NAC; Terrence Fretheim, NIB; John Walton, LAC; John E. Hartley, NIBC; Kenneth O. Gangel and Stephen J. Bramer, HOTC

Exodus—Walter Brueggemann, NIB; Glen S. Martin, HOTC; R. K. Harrison, WEC; Douglas Stewart, NAC; Terence Fretheim, Int

Leviticus—Mark Rooker, NAC; Walter Kaiser Jr., NIB; Gordan

Wenham, NICOT; Samuel Balentine, Int; Glen S. Martin, HOTC; E. Gerstenberger, OTL

Numbers—Thomas Dozeman, NIB; Glen S. Martin, HOTC; Timothy R. Ashley, NICOT; R. Dennis Cole, NAC; Dennis Olson, Int

Deuteronomy—Gordon McConville, Apollos; Eugene Merrill, NAC; Ronald Clements, NIB; Doug McIntosh, HOTC; Patrick Miller, Int; Christopher Wright, NIBC; Peter Craigie, NICOT; Richard Nelson, OTL; Mark Biddle, S&H

Joshua—David Howard, NAC; Richard Hess, TOTC; Marten Woudstra, NICOT; Trent C. Butler, WBC; Robert Coote, NIB; John Hamlin, International Theological Commentary; L. Daniel Hawk, Berit Olam; Jerome Creach, Int

Judges—Daniel Block, NAC; K. Lawson Younger, LAC; Trent C. Butler, WBC; Susan Niditch, OTL; Dennis Olson, NIB; A. E. Cundall, TOTC; E. J. Hamlin, International Theological Commentary; D. R. Davis, Such a Great Salvation, Baker; J. Clinton McCann, Int

Ruth—Daniel Block, NAC; K. Lawson Younger, LAC; Robert L. Hubbard, NICOT; Kathleen Robertson Farmer, NIB; Frederic Bush, WBC; Katharine Sakenfeld, Int

1 Samuel—Joyce G. Baldwin, TOTC; Walter Brueggemann, Int; Bruce Birch, NIB; Robert Bergen, NAC; Ralph Klein, WBC; Keith Bodner, Readings

2 Samuel—Joyce G. Baldwin, TOTC; Walter Brueggemann, Int; Bruce Birch, NIB; Robert Bergen, NAC

1 Kings—Paul House, NAC; Walter Brueggemann, S&H; Choon-Leong Seow, NIB; Iain Provon, NIBC; Marvin A. Sweeney, OTL

2 Kings—Paul House, NAC; Walter Brueggemann, S&H ; Choon-Leong Seow, NIB; Marvin A. Sweeney, OTL

1 Chronicles—Leslie Allen, NIB; M. J. Selman, TOTC; Roddy Braun, WBC; H. G. M. Williamson, NCB; J. G. McConville, Daily Study Bible; Sara Japhet, OTL; John Jarick, Readings

2 Chronicles—Leslie Allen, NIB; M. J. Selman, TOTC; Ray Dillard, WBC; H. G. M. Williamson, NCB; J. G. McConville, Daily Study Bible; Sara Japhet, OTL; John Jarick, Readings

Ezra—F. Charles Fensham, NICOT; Derek Kidner, TOTC; G. F. Davies, Berit Olam; H. G. M. Williamson, WBC; Ralph Klein, NIB; Ed Yamauchi, EBC; Joseph Blenkinsopp, OTL

Nehemiah—F. Charles Fensham, NICOT; Derek Kidner, TOTC; G. F. Davies, Berit Olam; H. G. M. Williamson, WBC; Ralph Klein, NIB; Ed Yamauchi, EBC; Joseph Blenkinsopp, OTL

Esther—Joyce G. Baldwin, TOTC; Sidnie White Crawford, NIB; Frederic Bush, WBC; T. K. Beal, Berith Olam; J. D. Levinson, OTL; Karen Jobes, LAC

Job—Carol Newsom, NIB; John Hartley, NICOT; Francis I. Andersen,

TBC; Norman Habel, OTL; Gerald Janzen, Int; Norman Whybray, Readings

Psalms—Gerald Wilson, LAC; Derek Kidner, TBC, 2 vols.; James L. Mays, Int; J. Clinton McCann, NIB

Proverbs—Raymond van Leeuwen, NIB; Roland E. Murphy, WBC; Duane Garrett, NAC; Leo Perdue, Int

Ecclesiastes—Tremper Longman III, NICOT; Duane Garrett, NAC; W. Sibley Towner, NIB; James Crenshaw, OTL

Song of Solomon—Tremper Longman III, NICOT; Duane Garrett, NAC; Cheryl Exum, OTL; Renita Weems, NIB

Isaiah—Gene Tucker and Christopher Seitz, NIB; Trent C. Butler, HOTC; J. N. Oswalt, NICOT; John Oswalt, LAC; C. Seitz, Int; Brevard Childs, OTL; Gary Smith, NAC; Peter Miscall, Readings

Jeremiah—Patrick Miller, NIB; Charles L. Feinberg, EBC; R. K. Harrison, TOTC; Leslie Allen, OTL

Lamentations—A. Berlin, OTL; Kathleen O'Connor, NIB

Ezekiel—Daniel I. Block, NICOT; Joseph Blenkinsopp, Int; Leslie C. Allen, WBC; Katheryn Pfisterer Darr, NIB; John B. Taylor, TOTC; Lamar Cooper, NAC;

Daniel—Tremper Longman III, LAC; John Goldingay, WBC; Ernest Lucas, Apollos; Joyce Baldwin, TBC; Daniel Smith-Christopher, NIB; Kenneth O. Gangel, HOTC

Hosea—Duane Garrett, NAC; David A. Hubbard, TOTC; Douglas Stuart, WBC; Gary Smith, LAC; Gale Yee, NIB; G. I. Davies, NCB; J. Limburg, Int ; Trent Butler, HOTC

Joel—Duane Garrett, NAC; Leslie Allen, NICOT; David A. Hubbard, TOTC; Douglas Stuart, WBC; Elizabeth Achtemeier, NIB; T. J. Finley, WEC; J. Limburg, Int; John Barton, OTL

Amos—Gary Smith, *Amos A Commentary*, Zondervan; David A. Hubbard, TOTC; Douglas Stuart, WBC; ; Gary Smith, LAC; T. J. Finley, WEC; Donald Gowan, NIB; J. Limburg, Int

Obadiah—Leslie Allen, NICOT; Douglas Stuart, WBC; T. J. Finley, WEC; J. Limburg, Int; John Barton, OTL; Samuel Pagán, NIB

Jonah—Douglas Stuart, WBC; Leslie C. Allen, NICOT; Phyllis Trible, NIB; James Limburg, OTL

Micah—Gary Smith, LAC; Leslie Allen, NICOT; Kenneth Barker, NAC; J. Limburg, Int; Daniel Simundson, NIB

Nahum—O. Palmer Robertson, NICOT; Elizabeth Achtemeier, Int; Waylon Bailey, NAC; R. D. Patterson, WEC; D. W. Baker, TOTC; Francisco García-Treto, NIB; Julia O'Brien, Readings

Habakkuk—O. Palmer Robertson, NICOT; Elizabeth Achtemeier, Int;

R. D. Patterson, WEC; Theodore Hiebert, NIB; Waylon Bailey, NAC; D. W. Baker, TOTC

Zephaniah—O. Palmer Robertson, NICOT; Elizabeth Achtemeier, Int; R. D. Patterson, WEC; D. W. Baker, TOTC; Robert A. Bennett, NIB; Waylon Bailey, NAC

Haggai—Pieter A. Verhoef, NICOT; Joyce Baldwin, TBC; Mark Boda, LAC; Elizabeth Achtemeier, Int; Eugene March, NIB; Richard Taylor, NAC

Zechariah—Joyce Baldwin, TBC; Elizabeth Achtemeier, Int; Ben Ollenburger, NIB; George Klein, NAC; Mark Boda, LAC

Malachi—Pieter A. Verhoef, NICOT; Joyce Baldwin, TBC; Elizabeth Achtemeier, Int; E. Ray Clendenen, NAC; Eileen Schuller, NIB

Matthew—Craig Blomberg, NAC; D. A. Carson, EBC; Donald Hagner, WBC; Eugene Boring, NIB; Stuart Weber, HNTC; Margaret Davies, Readings

Mark—David E. Garland, LAC; Robert Gundry, *Mark: A Commentary on His Apology for the Cross,* Eerdmans; Robert Guelich, WBC; Pheme Perkins, NIB; Larry Hurtado, NIBC; Eugene Boring, NTL

Luke—R. Alan Culpepper, NIB; I. Howard Marshall, NIGTC; Robert Stein, NAC; Joseph Fitzmyer, AB; Luke Timothy Johnson, Sacra Pagina; John Nolland, WBC; Fred Craddock, Int; Darrell Bock, LAC; Trent C. Butler, HNTC

John—Raymond Brown, AB; George R. Beasley-Murray, WBC; J. Ramsey Michaels, NIBC, Leon Morris, NICNT; Gerald Borchert, NAC; Donald Carson, Pillar New Testament; Gail O'Day, NIB; Kenneth O. Gangel, HNTC

Acts—John Polhill, NAC; F. F. Bruce, NIGNT; Bruce Witherington, *The Acts of the Apostles: A Socio-Rhetorical Commentary,* Eerdmans; Ajith Fernando, LAC; Robert Wall, NIB; Joseph Fitzmyer, AB; Kenneth O. Gangel, HNTC; Luke Timothy Johnson, Sacra Pagina

Romans—James D. G. Dunn, WBC; Douglas Moos, LAC; Ernst Käsemann, *Commentary on Romans,* SCM; Leon Morris, Pillar New Testament; Paul Achtemeier, Int; C. K. Barrett, Harper and Brothers; Douglas J. Moo, NICNT; Anders Nygren, *Commentary on Romans*; Karl Barth, *The Epistle to the Romans*; Joseph Fitzmyer, AB; Stanley Porter, Readings; N. Thomas Wright, NIB

1 Corinthians—Gordon Fee, NICNT; Craig Blomberg, LAC; Paul Sampley, NIB

2 Corinthians—Ralph Martin, WBC; David E. Garland, NAC; Scott Hafemann, LAC; Victor Paul Furnish, AB; Ernest Best, Int; Paul Sampley, NIB; Frank Matera, NTL

Galatians—Richard Longenecker, WBC; Scott McKnight, LAC; F. F.

Bruce, NIGTC; J. Louis Martyn, AB; Timothy George, NAC; James D. G. Dunn, Black's Commentary, Hendrickson; Richard Hays, NIB; Max Anders, HNTC; Charles B. Cousar, Int; Richard Donald Guthrie, NCB

Ephesians—Klyne Snodgrass, LAC; Ralph P. Martin, Int; Pheme Perkins, NIB; Andrew Lincoln, WBC; Markus Barth, AB; Max Anders, HNTC; Klyne Snodgrass, LAC; Peter O'Brien, Pillar; Richard Melick, NAC

Philippians—Frank Thielman, LAC; F. F. Bruce, NIBC; Gordon Fee, NICNT; Peter O'Brien, NIGTC; Morna Hooker, NIB; Max Anders, HNTC

Colossians—David E. Garland, LAC; James D. G. Dunn, NIGTC; P. T. O'Brien, WBC; Ralph Martin, Int; Ralph Martin, NCB; Andrew Lincoln, NIB; Max Anders, HNTC; Jerry Sumney, NTL

1 Thessalonians—Leon Morris, NICNT; I. Howard Marshall, NCB; Michael Martin, NAC; Charles Wanamaker, NIGTC; Beverly Gaventa, Int; Gene Green, Pillar; Abraham Smith, NIB

2 Thessalonians—Leon Morris, NICNT; I. Howard Marshall, NCB; Michael Martin, NAC; Charles Wanamaker, NIGTC; Beverly Gaventa, Int

1 Timothy—Gordon Fee, NIBC; G. W. Knight, NIGTC; C. K. Barrett, *The Pastoral Epistles,* Clarendon; Thomas C. Oden, Int; Donald Guthrie, TBC; Thomas Lea, NAC; Raymond Collins, NTL

2 Timothy—Gordon Fee, NIBC; G. W. Knight, NIGTC; C. K. Barrett, *The Pastoral Epistles,* Clarendon; Thomas C. Oden, Int; Donald Guthrie, TBC; Thomas Lea, NAC; Raymond Collins, NTL

Titus—Gordon Fee, NIBC; G. W. Knight, NIGTC; J. D. Quinn, AB; C. K. Barrett, *The Pastoral Epistles,* Clarendon; Thomas C. Oden, Int; Donald Guthrie, TBC; Raymond Collins, NTL

Philemon—James D. G. Dunn, NIGTC; F. F. Bruce, NIGTC; David E. Garland, LAC; Peter O'Brien, WBC; Ralph Martin, NCB

Hebrews—George Guthrie, LAC; Fred Craddock, NIB; F. F. Bruce, NICNT; William Lane, WBC; Donald Guthrie, TNTC; Paul Ellingworth, NIGTC; Donald Hagner, NIBC; Philip E. Hughes, *A Commentary on the Epistle to the Hebrews,* Eerdmans; Luke Timothy Johnson, NTL; David Allen, NAC

James—P. H. Davids, NIGTC; Luke T. Johnson, NIB; Luke T. Johnson, AB; Ralph Martin, WBC; Douglas Moo, Pillar New Testament

1 Peter—Thomas R. Schreiner, NAC; J. Ramsey Michaels, WBC; Pheme Perkins, Int; P. H. Davids, NICNT; N. Hillyer, NIBC; Scott McKnight, LAC; David L. Bartlett, NIB; Donald Senior and Daniel Harrington, Sacra Pagina

2 Peter—Thomas R. Schreiner, NAC; R. J. Bauckham, WBC; Duane Watson, NIB; Michael Green, NICNT; D. J. Moo, LAC; J. H. Neyrey,

AB; N. Hillyer, NIBC; Donald Senior and Daniel Harrington, Sacra Pagina

1 John—Raymond Brown, AB; Daniel L. Aiken, NAC; I. Howard Marshall, NICNT; Stephen Smalley, WBC; D. Moody Smith, Int; C. Clifton Black, NIB; Judith M. Lieu, NTL; Colin Kruse, Pillar New Testament

2 John—Raymond Brown, AB; Daniel L. Aiken, NAC; I. Howard Marshall, NICNT; Stephen Smalley, WBC; D. Moody Smith, Int; C. Clifton Black, NIB; Judith M. Lieu, NTL; Colin Kruse, Pillar New Testament

3 John—Raymond Brown, AB; Daniel L. Aiken, NAC; I. Howard Marshall, NICNT; Stephen Smalley, WBC; D. Moody Smith, Int; C. Clifton Black, NIB; Judith M. Lieu, NTL; Colin Kruse, Pillar New Testament

Jude—R. Schreiner, NAC; Jerome Neyrey, AB; Richard Bauckham, WBC; Michael Green, NICNT; D. J. Moo, LAC; Duane Watson, NIB; N. Hillyer, NIBC; Donald Senior and Daniel Harrington, Sacra Pagina

Revelation—Kendell H. Easley, HNTC; D. E. Aune, WBC; Robert H. Mounce, NICNT; Christopher Rowland, NIB; G. R. Beasley-Murray, NCB; George Eldon Ladd, *A Commentary on the Revelation of St. John,* Eerdmans; Leon Morris, TNTC; Eugene Boring, AB; G. K. Beale, *The Book of Revelation: A Commentary on the Greek Text,* Eerdmans; John F. Walvoord, *The Revelation of Jesus Christ,* Moody; Craig Keener, LAC; Jonathan Knight, Readings

Glossary

A

Aleppo Codex—Early Hebrew incomplete manuscript from about 950 C.E.

American Standard Version 1901—American revision of 1885 British official edition; extremely literal with very high reading level.

Anachronisms—Detail in a literary work that comes from chronological period of author rather than that of the story being told; placing a 2005 car in a movie about Franklin D. Roosevelt

Antithetical parallelism—Device in Hebrew poetry where second line of poetry says the opposite of first line.

Apocalypse— Final period of history; for Christians the second coming of Christ; literature focusing on apocalypse like Daniel and Revelation is called apocalyptic literature.

Apocrypha or deutero-canonical literature—Refers to books written between time of Malachi and of Jesus and regarded as part of inspired Scripture by Roman Catholic church and a afew other groups.

Aposiopesis—Literary device to mark silence caused by speaker's inability, lack of desire, or fear to speak

Aramaic—Language of trade and politics in later period of Old Testament and that of New; basic language of Jews at time of Jesus; language of parts of Ezra and Daniel.

Athanasius—Bishop of Alexandria in Egypt about 325 to 373 c.e.; listed the books in present New Testament canon.

Authorized version—Name for King James Version of Bible.

B

B19ᴬ—Official designation of Leningrad manuscript used for most editions of the Hebrew Bible text.

Babylon—Country at southern end of Euphrates River which controlled the Near East from about 609 b.c. to 538 b.c. Destroyed Jerusalem in 586 b.c. and took leading citizens into exile; see Psalm 137

Baruch—Scribe who assisted Jeremiah; works attributed to him are in Apocrypha

Battle reports—Literary form that gives basic details of a military encounter including marshalling of forces, the confrontation in battle, and the consequences.

Bel and the Dragon—Additions to the book of Daniel found in the Apocrypha.

Biography—Literary type that centers on the life and significance of an individual; to an extent Joshua provides biography of Joshua and the gospels present a type of biography of Jesus.

Bishops' Bible—English translation of the Bible in 1568 by bishops of Church of England.

Blessing—Literary form usually beginning with participle "Blessing" used to call down divine favor on an individual or group.

Bomberg Bible—Named after its publisher; was the First Rabbinic Bible and was published in Venice in 1516-17.

Boundary lists—A literary form listing geographical borders or limits as in Joshua 15—19.

C

Canon—A collection of works considered authoritative by a specific group. Protestant Christians believe the Hebrew and Greek Testaments with 39 and 27 books, respectively, form the authoritative Scripture or canon.

Characterization—A literary element by which the author reveals the nature or character of an individual within a literary work.

Cheltenham Canon—Important New Testament manuscript from North Africa about 350.

Chronological movement—Literary element by which author shows action through time in a literary work.

Codex Claromontanus—Manuscript from about 350 A.D. including four gospels, 10 letters of Paul (probably accidently omitting Philippians and Thessalonians), James, 1 and 2 Peter, 1, 2, 3 John, Jude, Barnabas, Revelation, Acts, Shepherd of Hermas, Acts of Paul, and Apocalypse of Peter.

Codex Sinaiticus—Greek manuscript from about 325 c.e. including translation of Hebrew Bible, the Apocrypha, and 27 books of Greek New Testament plus Epistle of Barnabas and Shepherd of Hermas.

Community lament or complaint—Literary form prevalent in Psalms and Lamentation expressing sorrow, anger, and complaints of God's people in communal worship; often includes wailing, mourning, and fasting, invocation of God by name, complaint, description of tragedy, reference to previous time of blessing, confession of sin or assertion of innocence, call to weep and wail, plea or petition for help, curse on enemies, acknowledgment of divine response, vow or pledge to sacrifice, hymnic elements or blessings, promise to give thanksgiving; see Psalms 3—7.

Concordance—Essential tool for Bible study keyed to a specific English Bible translation and providing occurrences of words in the Bible text and verse(s) where word is found; range in size and completeness from small concordance in back of a Bible edition to exhaustive concordance listing every word in translation and giving keys to the Greek or Hebrew word translated.

Concursive Inspiration—Belief concerning the Bible that claims Inspired Scriptures are at the same time divine and human words. Scripture has a dual authorship, being a product of God as well as of human authors.

Contemporary English Version—English translation of Scripture by the American Bible Society with contemporary language rather than church theological language with easy reading scale.

Council of Hippo—Official church gathering in 393 that named 27 books in New Testament canon but separated Hebrews from Pauline list.

Council of Laodicea—Official church gathering in 363 A.D. that named 26 canonical books in the New Testament, omitting Revelation.

Council of Trent—Official church gathering on April 8, 1546, that declared the Latin Bible the official Bible of the Catholic Church.

Coverdale's Bible—Early English translation of the Bible by Miles Coverdale in 1535; Coverdale also translated Cromwell's The Great Bible.

Cross references—Essential Bible study tool available in many editions of the Bible in center dividing columns of Bible text or in outside column of the text; provides information where the term or idea appears in other Bible passages; may include references to textual notes.

D

John Nelson Darby—Translated Bible for Plymouth Brethren in 1871 into French, German, and English; formative figure in dispensational and premillennial theology.

Dead Sea Scrolls—Biblical texts and texts used to regulate life in the Jewish Qumran wilderness community; oldest Hebrew biblical texts available to modern scholars; very fragmented and contain only a small percentage of the biblical text. See the collection in The Dead Sea Scrolls Bible by Abegg, Flint, and Ulrich.

Devotional Study—Type of Bible study seeking personal communication with God and personal application of Scripture to personal life; built on top of other ways to study the Bible.

Dittography—Textual study name for copyist's error caused by copying same text twice.

Docetic view of Scripture—Heresy that teaches that the human authorship of Scripture is only apparent or imaginative.

E

Ecclesiasticus—Wisdom book in the Apocrypha written by Jesus the son of Sirach imitating the Book of Proverbs and also called The Wisdom of ben Sira(ch) or simply Sirach.

Edom—Small country east of Dead Sea with lineage from Esau; they joined Babylon in destruction of Jerusalem in 586 B.C. See Psalm 137.

Emotional movement—Literary tool used by author to show change of feelings and moods in a character or in a group of characters. May replace chronological movement as tool used to express change and progress in a narrative or poem.

Entertaining narrative—Literary type of narrative whose principle purpose is to entertain but which can be used to teach difficult lessons; secondary tool used by authors of Jonah and of Joshua 2 and by Jesus in several of his parables.

Epic—A literary genre or form involving a lengthy narrative poem or narrative in elevated language centering on an ancient hero or decisive historical moment in a nation's history, for example, Homer's Odyssey or the Hebrew Bible's exodus narrative.

Epistle of Baruch—A book included in the Syriac translation but not included in the Protestant Bible or the Apocrypha; found as the last part of 2 Baruch.

Epistle of Jeremiah—Book found in the Apocrypha encouraging audience not to be afraid of idols.

Exegesis—The study of Scripture with an intent to explain its details within the context of the passage and within the expanded context of the biblical canon and to determine its original meaning and purpose.

F

Footnotes—Information provided by a particular Bible translation usually located at the bottom of a page of biblical text and noting parallel passages, textual differences, or alternate translations; to be distinguished from the center column or side column cross-references and from the study notes in a study Bible.

G

Genealogy—A literary form showing either one generation of a family or the family ancestry for a number of generations; may show only one family of ancestors or a more complete family tree.

Geneva Bible—English translation completed in 1570 and translated by William Whittingham; used by King James, by Shakespeare, by Bunyan, the Puritans, and the Pilgrims.

Genre—Literary term for a specific form or type of literature at home in specific sociological setting and utilizing a standard set of literary elements; see communal lament above as one example of a genre.

GOD'S WORD—Bible translation by a Lutheran group seeking literal translation but replacing church's theological vocabulary with supposed modern equivalents.

Greek Fathers—Greek-speaking leaders of the church up until 451 C.E. whose writings formed the basis of Christian orthodoxy; including Athanasius, John Chrysostom, Cyril of Alexandria, Basil the Great of Caesarea, Gregory the Theologian of Nazianzus, and Basil's brother, Gregory of Nyssa.

H

Healing report—Literary form or genre used to describe miraculous healing; includes introduction of person needing healing, removal from public scene; healing description; dismissal.

Hebrew—Language in which Old Testament was first written; language Israelites spoke.

Historical narrative—Literary form describing an event usually having a plot with narrative tension, complication, and resolution; usually connected with professional scribes.

Historical Study—Way to study the Bible with the intent to determine the historical context in which a narrative is told; lets you situate the Bible passage in the context of the larger world history of the times; reveals the tension and the decisions that biblical characters faced; finds out where things took place and how the geography and topography of the land affected the situation.

Holman Christian Standard—Bible Translation by LifeWay Christian Resources that seeks to provide readable, literal translation between New International and New American Standard; retains most of traditional church theological vocabulary.

Homoeoarchton—Textual study term for error made by copyist moving from one word to another with similar or same beginning.

Homoeoteleuton—Textual study term for error made by copyist moving from one word to another with similar or same ending, thus skipping intervening text. See Isaiah 16:8-9.

Inerrancy—Theological claim that the Bible's original manuscripts contained no errors and is completely true in all that it affirms, to the degree of precision intended by the author's purpose, in all matters relating to God and His creation.

Infallibility—Theological claim that the Bible is incapable of error and cannot deceive or mislead; Bible is truthful in matters relating to history, geography, and related matters.

Inspiration—Superintending influence the Holy Spirit exerted on the biblical writers so that the accent and interpretation of God's revelation have been recorded as God intended so that the Bible is actually the word of God.

Instructions—Literary type or genre usually in imperative mode providing teachings on the universal elements of life on earth.

Invocation—Element of literary forms in which the name of God is called on as the addressee of prayer.

Irony—Literary tool used to state one thing while meaning something else, often something totally opposite; something readers know that characters do not; Jesus' call of blessing on poor and teaching that last shall be first or Joshua's use of harlot as main character with confession of faith.

J

Jerome—Translator of the Latin Vulgate about 400 C.E. based on Hebrew manuscripts instead of Greek for Old Testament without inclusion of Apocrypha that Church added later. Jerome translated New Testament gospels, but others apparently translated most of the rest of the New Testament.

Josephus *Jewish Wars*—Chonicle of the war that destroyed Jerusalem, written by Josephus. The author was a former Jewish revolutionary turned collaborator of Vespacian, the general who lead the Roman invasion and eventually became Emperor.

Judith—Deuterocanonical book that tells the story of a Jewish heroine.

K

King James Version—English translation of the Bible published in 1611.

L

Laments—Literary form, common in the Psalms, where a person or a nation complains before God and asks for a divine intervention.

Laws—Literary genre that groups the different norms given by God to the children of Israel.

Leningrad Manuscript—One of the oldest manuscripts of the complete Hebrew Bible. See B19ᴬ.

Letters—Written communications from the early Christian leaders to the congregations and church leaders, addressing theological and pastoral problems. Also called "epistles", the letters constitute a NT literary genre.

LXX—Abreviation for the Septuagint.

M

Massoretes—Jewish scholars who corrected and annotated the textual reading of the Hebrew Scriptures.

Miracle story—Literary form that narrates how a miracle worker, acting as a divine agent, heals a sick person.

Mocking song—Literary form, common in prophetic literature, that satirizes a given situation.

James Moffatt—Translator of new version of English Bible in 1926 intending to give audience conteporary language they could read with pleasure and for profit.

MSS—Abbreviation for manuscripts.

MT—Abbreviation for Massoretic Text, the standard Hebrew Bible text used by most Bible translators and scholars. Central manuscript is Leningrad B19^A from about 1000 C.E.

N

Narrative Theme—Literary element writers use to inject purpose, meaning, and continuity into narrative.

New American Bible—Official Roman Catholic translation into English in 1970; provides smooth reading and understanding.

New American Commentary—Conservative, evangelical commentary on entire Bible by B&H.

New American Standard Bible (NASB)—Bible translation by Lockman Foundation that is quite literal with high reading level; good for depth Bible Study.

New English Bible (NEB)—Officially updated British translation with some interesting Old Testament readings based on Arabic cognates of Hebrew words.

New English Translation (NET)—English translation of the Bible done for computer usage; features extensive system of textual notes with constant computer updates.

New English Translation of the Septuagint (NETS)—Modern English translation of earliest Greek translation of Hebrew Bible along with Apocrypha.

New International Commentary on the New Testament (NICNT)—Conservative evangelical commentary from Eerdmans for preachers on all books of the New Testament.

New International Commentary on the Old Testament (NICOT)—Conservative evangelical commentary for preachers from Eerdmans on all books of the Old Testament.

New International Readers Version (NIrV)—Modification of New International Version of the Bible published by Zondervan for young children and new readers.

New International Version (NIV)—Extremely popular evangelical translation of the Protestant Bible from Zondervan and International Bible Society.

New King James Version (NKJV)—Updated version of authorized King James Version using translation principles and text used by King James but with extensive textual notes.

New Living Translation (NLT)—Scholarly update of popular Living Bible from Tyndale based on original Ken Taylor translation/paraphrase for children; dynamic equivalent removes much of church's theological language.

New Revised Standard Version (NRSV)—Updated version of Revised Standard Bible by World Council of Churches marked by gender neutral language featuring extensive use of brothers and sisters but more conservative in its use of text criticism.

Normative Scripture—Theological claim that the Scripture's power is not limited by temporal or contextual matters. The message of Scripture has binding authority for the contemporary church.

O

Old Testament Library (OTL)—Critical series of commentaries on the Old Testament being updated by new authors from Westminster John Knox.

Oral tradition—Means of preserving Israel's early narratives by family heads and professional story tellers constantly teaching the stories to the family, to the clan, and in tribal meetings.

P

Personal revelation—A theological view that understands revelation primarily as a personal experience or encounter with God in Christ. It focuses attention on the dynamic and personal characteristics of God's manifestation of Himself to men and women.

Peshitta—The standard Syriac translation of the Old Testament; origin unknown; first appears in quotations after 300 C.E.; includes several works not in the Protestant Bible—Wisdom of Solomon, Epistle of Jeremiah, Epistle of Baruch, Baruch; Bel and the Dragon, Susanna, Judith, Ecclesiasticus, 2 Baruch, 4 Ezra, 1–4 Maccabees, and Josephus Jewish Wars. Some Syriac Psalters contain Psalm 151 (from LXX) and 152–55, now known from the Dead Sea Scrolls.

Plea—Element of literary form of lament stating need and asking for divine help.

Plenary—Latin term meaning full; theological view that the Bible is inspired in all of its parts.

Poetic parallelism—Major characteristic of Hebrew poetry in which second line either repeats or notes precise opposite of previous line; at times three lines involved.

Point of tension—Tool narrative authors use to create a story line or plot by building to a crisis point where audience cannot tell how the problem can be solved and then easing down into resolution. See spies hanging from ropes in Joshua 2 or man seeing people like trees walking in Mark 8.

Progressive revelation—Theological claim that God's self-disclosure unfolds and develops over time, interpreting and amplifying the previous revelation but not contradicting it in any way.

Prophetic sayings—Literary genre encompassing all types of utterances prophets used to convey divine message; include prophecy of punishment; prophecy of salvation, announcements of prophetic signs; prophetic judgment speeches.

Propositional revelation—God's self-manifestation understood as information about God, including the divine interpretation of revelatory events.

Q

Q source—Scholarly reconstruction of supposed source used by Matthew and Luke, comprising material in both of those gospels but not in Mark.

Qumran—Settlement near Dead Sea where Jewish Essene community lived practicing a life of purity, cleansing rituals, and study of ancient writings and of teachings of their leader, the Teacher of Righteousness. See Dead Sea Scrolls above.

R

Resolution—Literary tool authors use to create narrative plot; involves moving from crisis and point of tension back to normal circumstances through resolving the complexities and crises of the plot.

Revelation—Christian claim that the one and only God chooses to let humans know the deity and does so through creation, scripture, personal experience, and supremely through the cross and resurrection of Jesus.

Revised English Bible (REB)—Update of New English Bible by British scholars; contains many thought-provoking readings.

Revised Standard Version—Update of American Standard Version reducing reading level, using updated linguistic tools, using too many scholarly readings without textual base; standard translation in scholarly world for many years until updated with NRSV.

Rheims-Douay Bible—Translation into English of Catholic version of Scripture based on Latin Vulgate with New Testament appearing in 1582 and Old Testament in 1609; remained standard Catholic translation for centuries.

Rhetorical question—Literary tool authors use to involve readers directly by asking a question and not answering it because answer is obvious.

Royal annals—Records produced and kept by royal scribes tracing royal activities, particularly battles, and praising the king. May be represented in Old Testament by sources referred to by author(s) of 1 and 2 Kings.

S

Samaritan—Member of religious community living near ancient Shechem; descendents of mixed race that lived in northern Israel after Assyrians put an end to the northern kingdom in 721 B.C.E.; use only their version of the Pentateuch as Scripture.

Samaritan Pentateuch—Holy Scriptures for the Samaritan community; contains only Genesis, Exodus, Leviticus, Numbers, and Deuteronomy and has different readings at places to emphasize Samaritan beliefs and practices.

Self-curse—Literary tool authors use, especially in poetry, to show person's absolute dedication to accomplish task in question. See Psalm 137.

Sensus Plenior—Latin term scholars use to indicate their belief that God intended a fuller meaning of a passage of Scripture although that fuller meaning was not clearly understood by the human author or the original hearers/readers.

Septuagint (LXX)—Earliest translation (about 300 or so) of Hebrew Bible into another language—Greek; included the Apocrypha; basis for many conclusions in textual study of the Hebrew Bible

Short story—Literary genre or type revealing the established character traits of a few people who may be fictitious or historical (Ruth, Jonah, possibly Joshua 2).

Special Revelation—Theologian's term for God's self-manifestation in a particular way to particular people at particular times and places as with Moses at the burning bush or Jesus on the cross (often contrasted or coupled with general revelation as seen in creation and available to all people at all times).

Structural marker—Narrative element that shows transition from one narrative to the next with change in place, time, or characters.

Study notes—Special section of a study Bible, usually at bottom of page, that gives interpretation and factual details about the passages on the particular page.

Susanna—Story added to Daniel in the Apocrypha in which young Daniel rescues Susanna from death sentence based on false adultery charges.

Synonymous parallelism—Poetic literary device in Hebrew poetry in which two (or even three) lines repeat the same theme or thought in different words. See Psalm 145.

Syriac—Language developed from Aramaic dialect between 100 and 300 C.E. Became widely used by churches in Syria and Mesopotamia; used for Syriac translations of Bible. See Peshitta.

T

Targum Onqelos (TarOnq)—Early Jewish translation of the Pentateuch into Aramaic with homiletic notes also included; popular in Babylon.

Taunt song—Literary genre or type of poetry in which a victorious group sarcastically makes fun of the victims. See Psalm 137:3.

Textual notes—Notes at bottom of page tied to a particular translation and showing major differences in early texts and translations of the Bible. NET and NKJV provide most extensive sets of textual notes.

The Living Bible—Tyndale's loose translation based on the NASB originally done for translator's children; updated into full scholarly translation in New Living Translation.

The Message—Eugene Peterson's paraphrastic rendering of Bible into modern jargon for NavPress. Excellent tool for introducing people to the biblical content but not suitable or intended for serious Bible study.

Theological Study—Way of studying the Bible that leads to understanding the main theme or message of a passage and comparing that to the teaching of elements of the same theme in other passages of Scripture.

Theopneustos—Greek term translated "divinely inspired" or God-breathed (2 Tim. 3:16), indicating that the Scriptures are the product of God's creative breath and thus divine.

Trinity—Christian doctrine of God that claims God is three persons—Father, Son, and Holy Spirit—in one Godhead and that each has the full essence of divinity.

William Tyndale—Christian martyr for translating the Bible; produced printed New Testament in 1525 in Hamburg, but Henry VIII made this translation illegal to read; issued Pentateuch, Psalms, Jonah, and Joshua to 2 Chronicles before his execution in 1536.

Typological intepretation—Type of biblical interpretation in which pesons, events, or things in the Old Testament are interpreted as foreshadowings of persons, events, or things in the New Testament.

V

Victory songs—Poetic literary type comprised of music sung, usually by women, to greet victorious soldiers returning home from war. See Exodus 15; Judges 5; Psalm 68.

Vow—Promise to take a particular action made under oath invoking God's name as witness. See Genesis 28:20-21; Judges 11:30-31; 2 Samuel 15:7-8; Psalms 22:25; 61:5,8; 107; 137:5-6.

Vulgate (Vulg)—Jerome's translation around 400 c.e. of Hebrew Old Testament from Hebrew and Gospels from Greek into Latin joined with remainder of New Testament seemingly by other translators; long the official version of the Catholic Church. See Jerome.

W

Wisdom of Solomon—Book included in the Apocrypha.

Wisdom poems—Literary works such as Proverbs 31; Psalm 1 using poetic form to instruct God's people on special topics.

Word Biblical Commentary—One of most in depth commentary series on whole Bible with extensive notes on textual study and literary study.

John Wycliffe—Christian martyr for translating Latin Bible into English in 1382.

Z

Zion—Popular name, especially in poetry for Jerusalem; meaning of the word is not known.

Bible Translations Quoted

CPSIA information can be obtained
at www.ICGtesting.com
Printed in the USA
LVHW030000260320
651208LV00001B/1